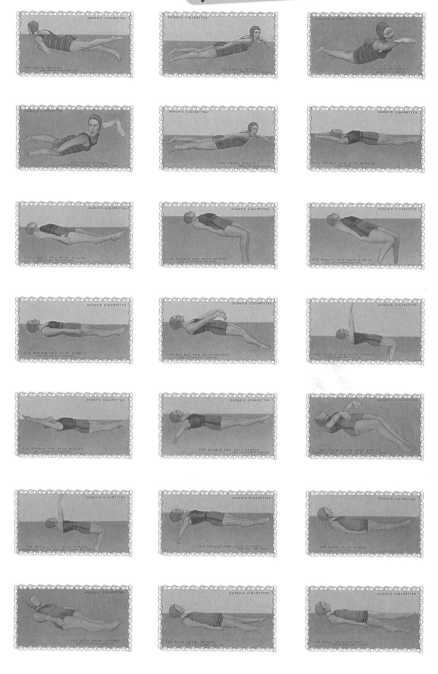

Swim

Swim

Why We Love the Water

Lynn Sherr

PublicAffairs
NEW YORK

Published in the United States by PublicAffairs™,
a Member of the Perseus Books Group

PublicAffairs books are available at special discounts for bulk purchases in
the U.S. by corporations, institutions, and other organizations. For more
information, please contact the Special Markets Department at the Perseus
Books Group, 2300 Chestnut Street, Suite 200, Philadelphia, PA 19103, call
(800) 810-4145, ext. 5000, or e-mail special.markets@perseusbooks.com.

Book design by Pauline Brown

Library of Congress Cataloging-in-Publication Data

Sherr, Lynn.
   Swim : why we love the water / Lynn Sherr.—1st ed.
      p.   cm.
   Includes bibliographical references and index.
   ISBN 978-1-61039-046-0 (hardcover)—ISBN 978-1-61039-047-7
(electronic) 1. Swimming—Psychological aspects. I. Title.
GV838.53.P75S44   2012
797.2'1019—dc23
                                                    2011044527

First Edition

Contents

Ancient Roman
provincial coin
showing Leander
swimming the
Hellespont

1

Diving In

THE SEA *surrounds me, a warm expanse of regal blue with gentle waves that barely stipple the surface. The calm is deceptive. I am trying to cut through a relentless cross-current with firm strokes of my own. Right arm, left arm, roll, breathe. The water lifts me; the land, another continent, seems distant. Relax, I tell myself. You'll make it.*

This is the Hellespont, known today as the Dardanelles, the storied channel separating Europe from Asia in western Turkey. Geographically, I am moving from one continent to the other, a passage more sensibly traveled by boat or plane. Historically, I am swimming at the threshold of what was once the known world. Ahead of me, on the eastern shore, lie the ruins of Troy, site of the decade-long war recounted in Homer's Iliad *that first confirmed the horrors of battle, an epic fought 3,200 years ago. Behind me rest the memorials to the men of both sides who died in the brutal Gallipoli campaign of World War I— the Swimmers' War, it's been called, for the innocents who bathed daily in the seas that soon ran red with their blood. These empty battlefields bracket centuries of conflicts over control of the waters that now buoy my body. Hittites, Mycenaeans, Greeks,*

Persians, Romans, Ottomans, Genoese, Venetians, Byzantines, Turks: all have ruled here. Achilles and Hector fought to the death for this fluid corridor; the Persian king Xerxes crossed it from Asia on a bridge of ships to invade the Greek settlements (after petulantly lashing the sea with whips when a storm destroyed his first attempt); Alexander the Great reversed direction to take them back. Jason sailed the Argo from here in search of the golden fleece; the fleece itself had swathed the flying ram on which Princess Helle escaped from her wicked stepmother. When Helle fell into this sea, it took her name: Sea of Helle, or Hellespont. History was transformed and empires crumbled in the wake of these mythic waters. The Hellespont has always been the route to something bigger—another conquest, another country, a new continent, a new adventure. And the legendary tale of tender new love.

Leander swims to Hero, waiting in her tower.

One summer evening, so long ago that the date has been lost, an energetic young fellow named Leander met a beautiful maiden named Hero and fell in love—"at first sight," as the poet Christopher Marlowe later wrote, thus delivering a lasting definition of romance. She was a priestess of Aphrodite, a virgin destined to remain chaste in her tower at Sestos, on the Greek shore; he was a townie from Abydos, on the Asian side. No way, said the elders; these waters exist to keep you apart. Which is not the sort of thing young lovers like to hear. So every evening, our hero, Leander, leapt into the water and swam across for a night of secret romance with his hero, Hero. She hung a lantern to light his way; he arrived gasping and briny, rank with the smell of fish. A few drops of rose oil, and they fell into bed together. At dawn Leander slipped back into the Hellespont to swim home, undetected. One night, the fury of approaching winter roiled the winds into a storm, dousing Hero's lamp. The sea spun, the waves roared, and Leander, unable to find his way, drowned. When his body washed ashore the next morning, Hero, overwhelmed with grief, jumped from her tower to join him in the afterlife. A double tragedy for this aquatic Romeo and Juliet. But their loss of life was folklore's gain: the doomed lovers became the costars of the most famous swimming myth in Western lore.

Leander drowns, in time-lapse artistry, as Hero falls to join him.

The poet George Gordon, better known as Lord Byron, himself a master swimmer with a fascination for all things classically Greek, was intrigued. Could it have happened? Was it possible to swim across these rough waters? On a Mediterranean journey in 1810, he decided to find out. Enlisting an officer from the frigate to join him, Byron made the crossing on his second try, establishing the Hellespont as a romantic challenge and becoming the poster child for overachieving swimmers around the globe. His companion, Lieutenant William Ekenhead, beat him across by five minutes but disappeared from the record books after he drowned during a drunken celebration of his promotion to captain some time later. Byron, on the other hand, boasted endlessly about his accomplishment and put the Hellespont at the top of the list of waterways he'd swum: London's Thames, Venice's Grand Canal, Switzerland's Lake Geneva. "I plume myself on this achievement," he wrote to a friend, "more than I could possibly do on any kind of glory, political, poetical, or rhetorical."

So what am I doing here on an August afternoon, 150 miles southwest of Istanbul, 5,000 miles from New York, my home? The Hellespont is a critical passageway, the final conduit of the unbroken flow from the Black Sea, south through the Bosporus and the Sea of Marmara on its way to the Aegean.

Nearly fifty thousand tankers and cargo ships funnel through here each year, one of the world's busiest and swiftest freight lanes. Mind the currents, I've been told, or I could get swept out toward Greece. Mind the critters, I've been warned: stinging jellyfish and other natural enemies also swim here. But its lure is magnetic. I, too, am

captivated by the classical world and have dusted off my college Greek to read up on the history; I, too, love to swim and am drawn by the passion of my predecessors. And at a stage of my life when I have more time to explore and mightier muscles to rely on, I, too, like a challenge and want to test my body and mind in these iconic waters. After years of tracing familiar routes at my own pace, what would it would be like to dip my toe into an alien ocean, to tackle a distance far beyond my longest laps? Will I find what blind Homer, writing some four hundred years after the Trojan War, called the "riptide straits" of the Hellespont or what Shakespeare (who never saw it either) dismissed as its "easy current"? Can I transfer years of paddling in perfect pools and lovely lakes and East Coast seashores to this wild strait dividing Europe and Asia? Can I, too, swim the Hellespont?

Swimming is my salvation. Ask me in the middle of winter, or at the end of a grueling day, or after a long stretch at the computer, where I'd most like to be, and the answer is always the same: in the water, gliding weightless, slicing a silent trail through whatever patch of blue I can find. Tell me, as the medical world does from time to time, to think of something pleasant and count backwards, and I'm back in the drink, enveloped by an ocean, a lake, or a turquoise box, carving long and languorous laps that lull me into serenity.

At one level, it's purely sensual: the silky feeling of liquid on skin; the chance to float free, as close to flying as I'll ever get; the opportunity to reach, if not for the stars, at least for the starfish. Swimming stretches my body beyond its earthly limits, helping to soothe every ache and caress every muscle. But it's also an inward journey, a time of quiet contemplation, when, encased in an element at once hostile and familiar, I find myself at peace, able—and eager—to flex my mind, imagine new possibilities, to work things out without the startling interruptions of human voice or modern life. The silence is stunning.

Have I mentioned that I'm a Pisces?

Over the years, I've managed to satisfy my cravings in an eclectic collection of international water holes. I've swum in an outdoor heated pool during a snowfall in Utah and from a black volcanic beach in Greece, in a stream-fed pond in the mountains of northern Kenya and in the cool aquamarine of a pool in the Australian desert. I've shared the sea with flabby Soviet matrons in the Crimea and alternated lanes with perfectly molded starlets in Beverly Hills. At a beach resort on Koh Samui, in the Gulf of Thailand, I had my choice of an infinity-edge pool with freshwater, a freeform version with salt water, and the gorgeous gulf itself. I have never had a bad swim. But I choose carefully. Once, planning a trip to Mongolia, I contemplated a dip in the cerulean depths of Lake Khuvsgul, a pristine alpine wonder about the size of New York's Long Island that is visible from the space station. It is the second largest lake in Asia (after Russia's Lake Baikal), supplying 2 percent of the world's freshwater, and I saw a perfect addition to my repertoire. What I hadn't planned on was the ice, still keeping the waters frigid in June. I kayaked instead.

Swimming is, in short, an obsession, benign but obstinate. "How do you get through the day if you can't throw yourself into water?" asks a character in playwright Richard Greenberg's *The American Plan*. And swimmer after swimmer tells me that she or he just doesn't sleep as well without a swim. That it restores their sanity—from the world, from their kids, from themselves. That it's not something they can skip. "I'm sure I'd be an alcoholic if I didn't have the swimming pool," says Esther Dyson, the high-tech guru and venture capitalist who has been swimming laps daily since she was eighteen. "It's my reset button." Over brunch, after that morning's swim, she tells me she used to write notes for her groundbreaking newsletter in between laps, keeping the paper dry on the bench. She still stays only at hotels with pools, posting an image of each on the web. Others turn up in her dreams. "Sometimes it's a moat, and I just keep swimming," she says. "Sometimes the pool is empty, just pavement. That's anxiety."

The lane line keeps us centered in more ways than one. The rhythm of our strokes brings order to our senses.

From a purely aesthetic view, swimming works magic. Henry James once said that the two most beautiful words in the English language are "summer afternoon." Add the word "swimming," and the day blooms even more grandly, especially if the fluid is as lucid as poet Anne Sexton described it:

Water so clear you could
read a book through it.

The British writer Charles Sprawson, whose elegant meditation *Haunts of the Black Masseur* has become a cult classic among the water-obsessed, defines the historical swimmer as "someone rather remote and divorced from everyday life, devoted to a mode of exercise where most of the body remains submerged and self-absorbed." Swimming, he writes, "appealed to the introverted and the eccentric, individualists involved in a mental world of their own." When I telephone him at his home in London to express my admiration, Sprawson confirms that he's describing himself. "Group swimming is not for me," he says. "I like swimming in odd places with legendary backgrounds." Like the Hellespont, which he's crossed twice. "It will be jolly nice," he encourages me before I go. "It will give you time to think."

Swimming forces you to focus and sets the mood to meditate; it allows you to dream big dreams. Silent film star and swimming champion Annette Kellerman, whose invention of the one-piece bathing suit in the early 1900s made women as agile as their male mates in the sea, wrote, "Swimming cultivates imagination; the man with the most is he who can swim his solitary course night or day and forget a black earth full of people that push." Or as Henry David Thoreau put it, we should each explore our "private sea, the Atlantic and Pacific Ocean of one's being alone."

Even the suggestion of swimming can be stirring. Watch a swimmer pass a building with a pool: the whiff of chlorine produces a wistful smile. Sit with swimmers when a TV commercial shows someone in the water: they actually stop and watch. "It's something where you can exert yourself and feel incredible afterwards," explains a former coach. "If you go out for a really hard run and give yourself the same exertion, you can't eat; you feel so miserable, all you want to do is cool off and drink. If you have a great swim workout, you want to go have a feast. Look at people's faces when they leave the athletic club: the ones who walk out looking like they feel great are the ones who just swam."

Swimmers are special, a swim mom tells me—so focused on their sport, so disciplined about their workouts, they have to do well in school. A former competitor says he used to resent it when he was introduced as "the swimmer" because it made him feel like an outsider. Now he's proud of it "because it takes a lot of commitment. And because I know that I can survive."

Swimming is brimming with idioms about our struggle for survival, about striving and thriving in an occasionally hostile world. Striking out as an iconoclast? You're swimming against the tide. Getting nowhere? You're treading water. Wrong about something? You're all wet. (That one's insidious; for many of us, wet can be wonderful.) How many times have you talked about "sticking a toe in" or "diving off the deep end" or finding yourself "in over your head"? And it's not just subprime mortgages that are "under water." We blithely refer to a change in circumstance as the "tide turning."

The real thing can stop you in your tracks, as one English Channel contender recently learned. Three hundred yards from the shore, after stroking his way through eighteen hours of turbulent waters, he was caught in a turning tide, a surge so powerful he couldn't chop through to the finish line. "It's mental torture," his coach, Fiona Southwell, tells me. "You have to dig deep." Southwell, a cheery blonde Brit who completed her own Channel crossing at age fifty-one to compensate for empty-nest syndrome when her children went off to college, gives me the secret to her nineteen-hour, twenty-two-minute achievement: "I tied an imaginary rope to the shore in Dover, where I began. The other end was tied to the beach in France, where my eighty-three-year-old parents would be waiting to meet me. Every stroke I took, I imagined pulling myself closer to them, and when I hit a wall my son reminded me not to let go until I stood on French soil. It worked! They were just pulling me in."

Life lessons from swimming permeate the foundations of our society, with references in everything from the Bible to rock music. In a fourteenth-century illuminated manuscript accompanying Psalm 69, King David—naked, a crown atop his curls—swims through an ocean of blue waves ("the deep waters" of despair), praying for salvation. The Talmud says that a Jewish father must do several things for his son: circumcise him, teach him Torah, find him a wife, teach him a trade. And teach him how to swim. According to Rabbi Anne Ebersman, director of Jewish programming at New York's Abraham Joshua Heschel School, that can be interpreted two ways: First, to prevent drowning in a world where trade depended on sea travel. "Ships were dangerous," she explains to me. "And probably there were stories about drowning. But swimming can also be seen more metaphorically," she goes on, "how to take care of yourself, knowing that you can master something by yourself. So it's a basic skill to get through life and also a metaphor to get through life." The same point is made by an advisor to Mohammed and one of the major voices of Islam, Umar Ibn al-Khattab. "Teach your children swimming, archery and horse-riding," he says, a directive often interpreted as serving the soul as well as the body.

More contemporary moral guidance comes from the bighearted blue fish named Dory in the movie *Finding Nemo*. When Marlin, the clownfish, gets the grumps, Dory grabs his fin, wriggles onward, and sings, "When life gets you down, do you wanna know what you've gotta do? Just keep swimming, swimming, swimming."

Andrew Grove, the genius behind Intel, called his memoir about escaping from war-ravaged Hungary *Swimming Across*. In it, he talks about his childhood—when he was known as Grof—and he relates the story of his favorite high school teacher, Mr. Volenski, addressing assorted parents at a school meeting. "Life is like a big lake," he tells them. "All the boys get in the water at one end and start swimming. Not all of them will swim across. But one of them, I'm sure, will. That one is Grof." Grove recalls that his parents "told so many people about [the story] that over time, my swimming across the lake of life became a family cliché. [But] I continued to get some encouragement from each telling. I hoped Mr. Volenski was right." He was. Grove got out. And up. He ends his memoir this way: "I am still swimming."

Me too. Which is what this book is about.

It's a celebration of swimming and the effect it has on our lives. It's an inquiry into why we swim—the lure, the hold, the timeless enchantment of being in the water. It's a look at how swimming has changed over the years and how this ancient activity is becoming more social than solitary today. It's about our relationship with the water, with our fishy forebears, and with (suck in your stomachs, class) the costumes that we wear. You'll even find a few songs to make the laps go by more quickly.

It's also about my progress in the Hellespont. Byron was twenty-two when he crossed it—in an hour and ten minutes. I assume that Leander's nocturnal outings took half as long, perhaps before he was sixteen. I vaguely remember both those birthdays and am hoping to finish before my next one removes me from my sixties. I've chosen this body of water carefully: wide enough to challenge me, reasonable enough to think I might make it. Might. I've airily assured friends that if I stop partway, it won't matter—just trying is enough. It's a bluff. I'm not used to failing. Never mind that I've swum no further than half a mile or so at a time for decades and that some of my strokes are unreconstructed leftovers from summer camp. I've trained hard for eight months, in pools and bays and oceans, plumbing my own untapped limits while chasing this more tangible goal.

Breaking the surface of anything is both thrilling and frightening—a body of water all the more so, as the ripples set off by our fingertips merely hint at the mystery of what lies below. And then it's as if you were never there. Water mends itself, sealing over the slightest intrusion so someone else—or you—can try again. There's an image that intrigues me: A young man painted on a tomb in ancient Paestum, in Italy, soaring headfirst into the water. Or wherever his final destination might be. You can't see his target, but his ease and elation are enviable. He trusts what he'll find, even though he can't be sure what it is. That's where I'm headed, too. If you're a swimmer, you know the feeling. If you're not, I hope you'll take a look, take some lessons, and dive in yourself. Swimming is magical. It can also save your life.

Diver's tomb, Paestum

The Skinny on Dipping

- An estimated 51.9 million Americans swim at least six times each year—one in six of us—making it the third most popular sports activity after walking and working out. A much smaller but far more dedicated group, 6.3 million, swim at least once a week for fitness or competition. That's a lot fewer than regular runners and bikers, perhaps because swimming requires five to ten times as much energy as crossing the same distance on land. Or maybe it's about getting your hair wet.
- We splash about in nearly 10.4 million residential pools and another 309,000 public pools across the country.
  - Of the four strokes most commonly used today—butterfly, back, breast, free—the fastest is free. It used to be called "crawl," a term an upcoming generation will likely stop using altogether, but not me. The two words are used interchangeably here.
  - Except for the breaststroke, arms are more important than legs in swimming, providing up to 80 percent of power.
  - The swimming pool at your local rec center is likely twenty-five yards long, which is called the standard Olympic short course. Internationally, yards become meters, which are slightly longer. The pool you see at the Olympics is fifty meters, which is called the long course. Most pools in American backyards are forty feet.

    How to measure your own laps? In a twenty-five-yard pool, 71 lengths equal one mile. In a forty-foot pool, 132 lengths equal one mile.

    The racing community measures it differently. To them, 66 lengths of a twenty-five-yard pool make a mile. Don't ask; it's a gift.

Percey, Many Swimmers

- Pools used to be called tanks, whether they were actual tanks full of water or just holes in the ground. What you wore in a tank was a tank suit. Brenda Patimkin wore a black one in Philip Roth's *Goodbye, Columbus*. Decades later, changing its name to "maillot" has not lessened the angst over fitting into one.

- Saltwater is more buoyant than fresh, cold water more than warm. Both will keep you afloat.
- The first person to swim the English Channel was Matthew Webb in 1875. First woman: America's Gertrude Ederle in 1926. Number of people who have swum the Channel to date: around nine hundred. Most jaw-dropping Channel feat (so far): a triple crossing (that's across, back, across again). I don't know why either.
- Weirdest swimming spin-off: underwater hockey.
- Best swim gear ever invented: goggles. Most annoying thing about swim gear: caps don't keep your hair dry.

Myths about swimming infuse many cultures. The one about Hero and Leander is about as fact-based as the ones about mermaids and mermen. Here are some more:

- A drowning person does not go down three times before succumbing. It could be only once. Or thirty-three.
- Witches do not float better than regular people, despite the devilish punishment devised by ignorant authorities in times past. They called it "swimming the witch"—dunking the accused, who was trussed like a chicken and often weighted down, in a body of water. If she stayed aloft, she was guilty and died; if she sank, she might die anyway.

The Swimming of Mary Sutton, 1613

- Eating before swimming is not recommended, but it will not cause you to drown. You do not have to wait one hour before plunging in. But don't tell your kids. Better they should digest.
- Contrary to urban legend (and an episode of *The Adventures of Pete & Pete* on Nickelodeon that revolved around "a chemical agent that reacts with human tinkle" and turns into a green slick), there is no known chemical that turns green, or any other color, when it comes in contact with bodily fluids in the pool. Unfortunately.

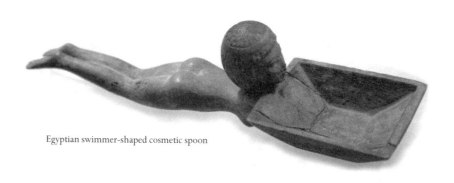

Egyptian swimmer-shaped cosmetic spoon

2

Water Babies

W E SWAM before we walked or breathed, but then we forgot. Over and over again. The same thing happened outside the womb: swimming was practiced regularly in ancient times but virtually disappeared for centuries. It finally resurfaced in the modern world, rising and falling like a wave and periodically getting rediscovered. If only we'd paid attention to the handwriting on the wall.

Egyptian hieroglyph

Thousands of years ago in Egypt, swimming was so familiar, there were several hieroglyphs for it. Fashionable ladies applied their makeup from long, slender spoons sculpted like a female swimmer's body.

And on the walls of the so-called Cave of the Swimmers in the Eastern Sahara, images of plump bodies jauntily stroke through the prehistoric waters that once irrigated the area. The goldfish-sized figures, relics of an era before climate change dried up their sea, are the real-life version of the memories invoked by the wounded airman in Michael Ondaatje's *The English Patient*, a dreamy fusion of time past and present. The author chose the granite grotto as his backdrop, he told me, "because it seemed so primal: swimming in the desert." At least one archaeologist suggests that the blissful figures may be gliding to the underworld, not the next beach, but even that would have required knowledge of strokes.

In other words, there wasn't one of those first-brave-person-to-eat-an-oyster moments.

S wimming was so deeply embedded in the culture of classical Greece, Plato quotes the proverb, well known in 360 BCE, that calling men ignorant means "they know neither how to read nor how to swim." Alexander the Great rued the ignominy. "Most miserable man that I am," he lamented, as his Macedonian troops faced a wide river before an enemy citadel, "Why, pray, have I not learned to swim?" For Socrates, it was a critical life skill. Swimming, he said, "saves a man from death."

Ancient coin showing
Aphrodite swimming

That the men of antiquity addressed themselves only to other men didn't stop many women—real and imagined—from doing as they pleased. The Theban princess Semele, who holds special status in Greek mythology as the only mortal parent of a god (Dionysus), was a graceful and accomplished swimmer who could glide across a rapid stream without getting her hair wet and wash off the terror of dreams with one plunge into the water. A group of young Amazons—those too-good-to-be-true women warriors—are painted sliding through the sea on a red and black vase, sharing an afternoon of pleasure with a pair of equally serene fish. Two bathing caps hanging from unseen hooks remind us how little things change.

Swimming converted young men into heroes. Roman noblemen taught their sons how to swim, a lesson in the manly arts. The centaur Chiron trained Achilles, in an age when the storied acts of immortals reflected the earthly activities of humans. And a compelling section from *The Odyssey* is a portrait in heroism. Odysseus is trying to find his way home—after ten years of war at Troy and seven of sea travel—when Poseidon stirs up a battering storm. The weary warrior is tossed into the wine-dark waters for more than two days. A friendly goddess gives him a life-saving scarf, and Athena calms the winds, but what ultimately powers Odysseus through the murderous waves is his own extraordinary skill. He "dove headfirst into the sea," Homer tells us, "stretched out his arms, and stroked for life itself."

Swimming was also one of the martial arts.

A series of reliefs from the ninth century BCE depicts the battle of Nineveh in ancient Assyria, near modern-day Mosul in northern Iraq. The warriors exhibit an impressive range of aquatic skills: one muscular fellow with bulging biceps tows a boat full of people; several others steal across the water atop inflated goat skins called *mussuks*,

Armed Assyrians cross a river on *mussuks*, accompanied by fish.

Detail of underwater warriors on a Chinese bronze vessel, dating from the fifth to fourth centuries BCE

the inner tubes of antiquity, packing quivers and shields on their backs; a raft of reserves prepares to join the invasion. All this while dodging schools of fish, some of them human-sized.

Further east and many centuries later, a Chinese bronze from the turbulent Warring States Period depicts a fierce naval battle. Two ships face off, prow to prow, as seamen onboard fight with long spears and short swords. Shift your gaze below deck, way below deck, and you find three lithe swimmers ready for combat beneath the hulls. These early precursors of our Navy SEALS are among the first depictions of human swimmers in China. Once again, giant fish authenticate the tableau.

In Greece, at least one major military victory is chalked up to swimming. During the Persian War, in 480 BCE, a noted diver named

Scyllias and his talented daughter Cyana (or Hydna) swam underwater to cut the anchor lines of the Persian ships in the Bay of Salamis. The chaos that followed led to pitched warfare and Greek triumph, not least because of their mismatched aquatic skills. "Of the Greeks there died only a few," wrote Herodotus, "for, as they were able to swim, all those that were not slain outright by the enemy escaped from the sinking vessels and swam across to Salamis. But on the side of the Barbarians more perished by drowning than in any other way, since they did not know how to swim." Not every part of the story holds up. Legend says the talented Scyllias then swam underwater to report his success to the Greeks at Artemisium, some eight miles distant. "In my opinion," Herodotus writes, "he came by boat."

In Rome, Publius Horatius Cocles famously held off the Etruscan invasion single-handedly while his colleagues destroyed the bridge over the Tiber. Then he swam to safety, a heroic crossing while gravely wounded, bearing full arms; he lost neither them nor his life. No less audacious was the later female version, when a young Roman named Cloelia escaped the same Etruscan aggressors by leading her sister hostages to freedom in a daring swim across the Tiber. Both stories are likely legendary, but that is beside the point; swimming was part of the conversation in Rome, a symbol of valor and a mark of respect.

The most prominent Roman to swim for the glory of the Republic was Julius Caesar. During the revolt against him in Alexandria, he tore himself away from Cleopatra and, ducking swords and Egyptian ships, "threw himself into the sea and with great difficulty escaped by swimming," according to Plutarch. Historians note that Caesar, then in his fifties, swam nearly three hundred meters—that's six lengths of an Olympic pool—clenching his sword and his purple cloak in his teeth, his papers held high above his head. As a result of his one-armed sprint, Ptolemy was slain and Cleopatra declared queen of Egypt.

While Caesar wisely removed his cloak to facilitate his escape in Egypt, swimming with heavy metal became a symbol of Roman pride. Scipio Africanus taught each of his soldiers to "stem the billows of the sea with his breastplate on," an awkward but handy trick. Their role models were Germanic tribesmen, known to ford the most turbulent streams clad head to toe in iron. By the fourth century CE, the author Vegetius recommended that the entire army be trained to swim, and included in his text a helpful, if not improbable, illustration of a fully sheathed soldier marching along the floor of the river with only his sword clearing the surface. How he was to breathe was not explained. The nearby fish have no such problem.

Unlikely wardrobe for a Roman swimming soldier, from Vegetius

Soldiers stayed submerged through the next millennium. The fictional Beowulf spent seven nights in the sea in a coat of mail, while balancing up to thirty changes of armor. Sir Lancelot, King Arthur's bold knight of the round table, faced a similar challenge, but claimed he could pull it off with ease, as reimagined in the Broadway show *Camelot*. In the charmingly arrogant "C'est Moi," his character boasts that being "invincible" meant one of his "impossible deeds" was to "swim a moat in a coat of heavy iron mail"— a coat weighing at least fifty pounds. Even Lancelot understood that was as daunting as slaying a dragon, with potentially mortifying results. Lancelot's colleague Sir Gawain, clad in a helmet and iron greaves, once tumbled into the deep water surrounding Lady Guinevere's castle and bobbed around helplessly. "One moment he rises, and the next he sinks," wrote Chrétien de Troyes, describing the other warriors' efforts to retrieve him. "One moment they see him, and the next they lose him from sight." The hapless Gawain was finally fished out with long hooks and branches, a soggy, silent knight.

That's how swimming moved to the Middle Ages, as a military function. It mostly took place in moats, which were designed to keep people out. Some historians blame its decline on the church, which censured everything from the revelries of Rome to the curves of the human body. Some say the ban on mixing water and flesh—even bathing was seen as a pagan ritual—was due to misguided medicine, with terrifying warnings of diseases lurking in contaminated water. The ignorance and charges of immorality worked. With rare exceptions, swimming vanished as Europe plunged into intellectual darkness.

It reappeared with the dawn of the Renaissance.

The first mention of swimming in print in Britain came in 1531, when Sir Thomas Elyot, a scholar who also coined the term "encyclopedia," wrote *The Boke, Named the Governour*, a popular guide for wannabe English gentlemen. "There is an exercise," he wrote (I've updated the English for easier reading), "which is right profitable in extreme danger of wars, but because there seems to be some peril in the learning thereof; and also it has not been of long time much used, especially among noble men, perchance some readers will little esteem it." Here's the payoff in the original English: "I meane swymmynge."

Seven years later a Swiss-German language professor named Nikolaus Wynmann published the world's first full book on swimming, *Colymbetes* (*The Swimmer, or the Art of Swimming*), a conversation in which Pampirus (the elder) teaches Erotes (the younger) how to swim. It is the first printed description of strokes, the first suggestion that swimming can open the wonders of the world. But since it was written in Latin, its impact was limited. One translator, however, has preserved a felicitous phrase that I'd nominate for swimming idiom of the century. When the lesson is over, Pampirus invites Erotes home with him so that they may get "an inward wet." An inward wet. It is a concept perhaps invented by the Roman poet Horace, who satirically described advice to cure insomnia: "Let those who are in need of deep sleep, anoint themselves [with oil] three times and swim thrice across the Tiber. Then, as evening falls, refresh themselves with wine." That's both an inward and outward wet.

All this was mere preface to the real breakthrough. In 1587, a cleric and philosophy scholar named Everard Digby wrote a tiny guide called *De Arte Natandi* (*On the Art of Swimming*) to rescue swimming "from the depths of ignorance and the dust of oblivion." The importance of this five-by-seven-inch volume on the history of swimming cannot be overestimated. For the first time in the modern era, swimming was being taught as a sport, a skill, and recreation—as *fun!*—something to do for its own sake, not just to repel the enemy. Saving lives was one motive, of course; England's coastal waters, swift rivers, and lakes took a huge toll yearly. Digby aimed to preserve human life from "the greedie jawes of the swelling Sea." But he wanted more than just attention to what he called "a thing necessary for every man to use." Addressing what he knew was a skeptical audience—he also wrote in Latin, the language of the establishment— he aimed to be to the art of swimming what Hippocrates and Galen were to the art of medicine, Aristotle to the liberal arts, Mercator to the maps of the world. Digby claimed boldly that humans (defined, in those days, as "man") swim naturally, even better than fish. As one of his later translators put it, "a man may swim with his face upwards, downwards; on his right side, on his left side; stand, sit, lie, carry his clothes and other things safely, walk in the bottom of the waters: which no fishes nor other creature can do." At a time when open water was the only option, he imparted such practical advice as this: swim only in daylight and only in summer months; don't swim in "a place growing full of weeds or grass." And look for clear water, "not troubled with any kind of slimy filth." Digby taught a swimmer how to flip from one side to the other, an invaluable skill should a ship suddenly appear "to run over him. . . . Likewise if there should be any Lions, Bears, or fierce dogs lurking in the river." He also may have been the first to advocate the buddy system, shrewdly suggesting that a beginner find a partner "taller and stronger than himself." Reverend Digby was so convinced of the benefits of swimming, he gilded his 114-page treatise with forty-three charming woodcuts illustrating techniques for taking the plunge. For example, here's how to enter the water, wading in slowly from the bank:

Here's how to do the backstroke:

Digby even anticipated the show-off kid on the high dive with some tricks you could perform in the water. Here is how to pare your toenails in the water—considerably easier than on the land, or in bed, he writes. As an added benefit, "you may easily wash your Toes."

Today, fewer than ten known copies of Digby's little treatise exist in the rare book collections of major libraries. Another sold in 2007 for more than $150,000. But while mesmerizing to us for its quaint yet precise understanding of the benefits of swimming, it too could have been read by only a few educated people. The author died shortly before another Everard Digby was famously executed for his role in the failed gunpowder plot to assassinate the king—what is now celebrated as Guy Fawkes Day. The conspirator was likely a distant relative, but as one British royalist and swimming aficionado later sniffed, he was guilty of a crime "of which no swimmer would be capable."

Still, while *De Arte Natandi* went largely unrecognized in Tudor England, it eventually found its audience. By 1696, more than a century after his little tome was first published, it had been shortened and translated twice into English and once into French. Unfortunately, two of the translators barely credited him, which is why his name was largely lost in history. But the message was spreading. When the French version, by Melchisédech Thévenot, librarian to King Louis XIV, was translated into English, it so caught the draft of the growing activity that it became, according to one historian, "the most popular book on swimming in France and England."

One of M. Thévenot's biggest swimming fans was an American teenager working as a printer in early-eighteenth-century London. "I had from a Child been ever delighted with this Exercise, had studied and practis'd all Thevenot's Motions and Positions," wrote Benjamin Franklin in his *Autobiography* many years later. He learned well, mastering "the graceful and easy, as well as the Useful," often demonstrating his talent. Once on a boat ride, Franklin was persuaded by friends to strip down and leap into the Thames, where he swam "from near Chelsea to Blackfryars," three and a half miles, "performing on the Way many Feats of Activity both upon and under the water, that surpriz'd and pleas'd those to whom they were novelties." Franklin also invented what may have been the first swim paddles—"two oval pallets, each about ten inches long, and six broad, with a hole for the thumb. . . . They much resemble a painter's pallets."

Franklin wrote that swimming cured everything from diarrhea ("I speak from my own experience") to insomnia ("After having swam [*sic*] for an hour or two in the evening, one sleeps coolly the whole night, even during the most ardent heat of summer"). And that's without Horace's cup of claret. He advised everyone to learn. One nobleman was so impressed with Franklin's skills, he offered him a handsome fee to instruct his own two sons. "From this Incident," Franklin later wrote, "I thought it likely, that if I were to remain in England and open a Swimming School, I might get a good deal of Money. And it struck me so strongly, that had the Overture been sooner made me, probably I should not so soon have returned to America."

Lucky for the young republic, he did.

What he found on this side of the pond was nothing like what he'd seen in London. At a time when there were no American swimming books and virtually no swim instruction, only a few colonists braved

They Call It
Windsurfing, Ben

"The exercise of swimming is one of the most healthy and agreeable in the world," Ben Franklin wrote, but he acknowledged that "rowing with the arms and legs" could be "a laborious and fatiguing operation when the space of water to be crossed is considerable." His solution:

When I was a boy, I amused myself one day with flying a paper kite; and approaching the bank of a pond, which was near a mile broad, I tied the string to a stake, and the kite ascended to a very considerable height above the pond, while I was swimming. In a little time, being desirous of amusing myself with my kite, and enjoying at the same time the pleasure of swimming, I returned; and, loosing from the stake the string with the little stick which was fastened to it, went again into the water, where I found that, lying on my back and holding the stick in my hands, I was drawn along the surface of the water in a very agreeable manner. Having then engaged another boy to carry my clothes round the pond, to a place which I pointed out to him on the other side, I began to cross the pond with my kite, which carried me quite over without the least fatigue, and with the greatest pleasure imaginable. I was only obliged occasionally to halt a little in my course, and resist its progress, when it appeared that by following too quick, I lowered the kite too much; by doing which I occasionally made it rise again— I have never since that time practiced this singular mode of swimming, though I think it not impossible to cross in this manner from Dover to Calais. The packet-boat, however, is still preferable.

the waters of Virginia's James River, Boston's Charles, Philadelphia's Schuylkill, among others. President John Quincy Adams took daily dips in the Potomac at 5 AM—naked—a practice so unusual it inspired a tale that made its way, more than a century later, into a White House press conference. President Harry S. Truman liked to tell the story, totally unsubstantiated, of Anne Royall, America's first female professional journalist, who was frustrated with her attempts to get an interview with President Adams. One day she supposedly followed him to the river, gathered his clothes, and sat on them until he answered all of her questions. "I thought you would be interested in that," Truman teased another insistent journalist, May Craig of the Portland, Maine, *Press Herald.* He, like Adams, is said to have admired the woman's spirit.

The real story about Adams's famous swims threatened considerably more than his dignity. One June day in 1825, he headed off on a little boat down Tiber Creek, which ran behind the White House to the Potomac. He was planning to paddle across (clothed) with his valet, Antoine Giusta, then swim back home. But a freak wind and sudden storm flooded the flimsy craft; when it sank, Adams and Giusta swam furiously for the opposite shore. Giusta made it easily since he had left his clothing behind, but the president was nearly dragged to the bottom by his long sleeves and trousers. As he later recorded in his diary, "while struggling for life and gasping for breath, [I] had ample leisure to reflect upon my own discretion." Adams gave his soggy garments to the valet and sent him to walk back for help. He then sat stark naked for five hours, separated from the Oval Office by more than half a mile of churning waters. A carriage finally returned him home, thus eliminating Vice President John C. Calhoun's chance to run the country. "By the mercy of God our lives were spared," President Adams wrote. At the insistence of his wife, Louisa, Adams discovered the joys of gardening. Today what remains of Tiber Creek runs under Constitution Avenue.

PRESIDENTIAL POOL REPORT

Presidential swimmers after John Quincy Adams include outdoorsman Theodore Roosevelt (who also skinny-dipped in the Potomac, and "swam Rock Creek in the early spring when the ice was floating thick upon it"), the very athletic Gerald Ford (who commissioned the outdoor pool at the White House), the former lifeguard Ronald Reagan (who reportedly saved seventy-seven lives on that job), and the famously buff Barack Obama, whose shirtless image wading into the Hawaiian surf in 2008 led to such a frenzy of tabloid headlines—PEC-TACULAR PRESIDENT-ELECT, for instance—the White House limited his exposure on the next outing. When he dove into Florida's waters in 2010, the press had to make do with a modest picture from a staff photographer.

In 1933, a White House laundry room was converted into a swimming pool so that the polio-stricken president Franklin Delano Roosevelt could get some exercise. President John F. Kennedy used it for noontime naked swims, partly to relieve his chronic back problems. In 1969 it was bricked over by President Richard Nixon (once photographed walking the beach in shoes and socks) to make, ironically, a press room. Today the tiled pool remains below, empty and unused. The podium where the press secretaries, or other members of the administration, are offered up to reporters, is located directly over the deep end. I told you swimming was a metaphor for life.

While Americans struggled with the proper way to enjoy the water, swimmers from other cultures practiced the art with natural grace. Numerous images capture the facility with which natives of Polynesia and the Caribbean dove for pearls or hunted for food. In *Typee*, his novel based on several months in the South Pacific, author Herman Melville describes the swimming skills of the women of the Marquesas: "Sometimes they might be seen gliding along just under the surface, without apparently moving hand or foot; then throwing themselves on their sides, they darted through the water, revealing glimpses of their forms, as . . . they shot for an instant partly into the air; at one moment they dived down deep into the water, and at the next they rose bounding to its surface."

Native Americans were also expert swimmers, as the artist George Catlin observed at a Mandan village on the upper Missouri. "They all learn to swim well," he wrote, "and the poorest swimmer amongst them will dash fearlessly into the boiling, and eddying current of the Missouri, and cross it with perfect ease. . . . It is learned at a very early age by both sexes, and enables the strong and hardy muscles of the squaws to take their child upon the back, and successfully to pass any river that lies in their way." A group of Minataree women, he wrote, swam "as confidently as so many otters or beavers . . . with their long black hair floating about on the water."

Africans from many tribes impressed legions of travelers with their effortless strokes. In 1454, one group of West Africans churning through the waves led Venetian explorer Cadomosto to call them "the best swimmers in the world." The eighteenth-century Scottish explorer Mungo Park had an African guide named Isaaco. He was swimming across a river when a huge crocodile clamped onto his thigh. As the story was reported at the time, the croc "would doubtless have crushed and torn it off with his immense jaws, but the negro was as good a swimmer and diver as the crocodile; and, turning rapidly round, he dashed his thumbs into the animal's eyes and

Dongola men of North Africa crossing a cataract

tore them out." When the animal seized his other thigh, Isaaco repeated the punishment. The croc finally let go, and Isaaco swam to safety, where Park dressed the wounds to complete the rescue.

Stories like these were read avidly in Europe, where the craze finally took hold. The nineteenth century was the swimming century, as men and women started flocking to the seashore. What began as a health movement—public baths to cleanse the great unwashed—soon became a sports mania. Clubs were established, along with competitions, some in indoor swimming pools. Swim schools opened in Paris, in Vienna, and across Europe. If you couldn't make it to class, there was a raft of instructional books, most still plagiarizing the pioneering Reverend Digby, some actually providing valuable new information. By the 1930s, lessons on each stroke were helpfully provided on wallet-sized cards given out with packs of cigarettes. There were no helpful hints on how to stop smoking.

In 1878, the Royal Navy, for the first time, required all seamen to know how to swim. And more than two millennia after Vegetius's attempt to steer armed soldiers through the water, a French cavalry officer named Vicomte de Courtivron figured out how to keep their powder dry. He invented a steel helmet with special clamps to grip the butt end of a rifle and a hook to fasten the trigger guard. Since the helmet was perched on the soldier's head, and since that head would best remain out of the water to inhale oxygen, the ingenious design also protected the bayonet and the cartridges.

Courtivron's contraption, clear of the water

M. de Courtivron demonstrated his headgear in the Seine one day, entering the river in full infantry garb, then loading and firing his weapon fourteen times despite the swift current. At least one newspaper called the exercise an "aquatic feat" and paired it with a report about two unadorned swimmers covering fifteen miles in Liverpool. The era of water spectacles had emerged, and the public thirst was unquenchable. London audiences flocked to the Thames to cheer on fourteen-year-old Agnes Beckwith, who was from a celebrated swimming family, as she churned through five miles of unfriendly waters from London Bridge to Greenwich in just over one hour, seven minutes—a new record. Another young female swimmer demolished her time several days later. At the Alhambra Theatre of Varieties, teenage star Elise Wallenda, of the Flying family, stayed submerged for four minutes and forty-five seconds in a glass-fronted tank, during which time she also undressed, wrote on a slate, sewed, and ate grapes. "There is one great objection to this feat," wrote an observer, "and that is the exceedingly grave liability to serious or fatal injury." Young Ms. Wallenda emerged unconscious but was revived. An Italian who billed himself only as Succi epitomized the extreme lengths to which swimmers would go to please their hydrophilic fans. He fasted for weeks and on at least one occasion then went to the Royal Aquarium to swim. So did his followers, to watch. Swimming was not only in but inane.

The bar was raised even further in 1875, when a stocky British sea captain named Matthew Webb, a self-described water lover who had read with interest the accounts of Byron's adventure across the Hellespont, swam what was considered unswimmable: the English Channel. The twenty-one-mile corridor between England and France was the biggest prize of all, the Mount Everest of the swimming world. Caesar had sailed it in 55 CE, bringing swimming and public baths to the British Isles. Now Webb crossed in the other direction, using the then-popular breaststroke to become an international star. In twenty-one hours and forty-five minutes—a grueling grind in egg-beater, grey-green water with inhuman tides that increased his distance to thirty-nine miles—Webb conquered not just the Channel but every famous swimmer before him. *Punch*, the British humor magazine, celebrated his success with a neat pun:

> Hurrah for daring Captain Webb,
> that resolute Commander!
> He has far outdone Lord Byron,
> Mr. Ekenhead, and Leander.
> As for Leander, now his fame must
> sink to nearly zero;
> For what is he compared with Webb—
> who's in himself a Hero?

Captain Matthew Webb

Webb's accomplishment seared his name onto the English consciousness and drew an eager crowd to every public bath. Boys across England clamored for swimming lessons and then swarmed into its ponds and streams.

By the time the sport debuted in the first modern Olympics, in 1896, champion swimmers were celebrities, and the sport had exceeded its origins.

The United States cannonballed in during the twentieth century. The appeal of swimming had spread in ever-widening ripples, from the soft-sand beaches of the Northeast to the palm-shaded turquoise of Florida and Southern California. Coney Island and Atlantic City were resorts, not just swimming holes, with live bands to swim by. Municipal pools made swimming available to the masses; exotic designs became Hollywood luxuries. And a nineteen-year-old New Yorker with a slick crawl and a winning grin swept swimming into the stratosphere. In 1926, Gertrude Ederle became the first woman to swim the English Channel, setting a speed record for both genders that would hold for twenty-four years. In Manhattan, 2 million people turned out for the biggest ticker tape parade the city had seen. Across the country, more than 60,000 women earned swimming certificates from the American Red Cross.

Gertrude Ederle, the first person to cross the Channel swimming the crawl

A new wave of American athletic stars floodlit popular culture: Johnny Weissmuller, Buster Crabbe, Esther Williams, Eleanor Holm. They smashed world swimming records and then lit up the silver screen. Aquacades—a new word for a splashy new form of entertainment—enchanted millions of Americans, with superstar swimmers appearing on stage behind curtains of water.

"Swimming was the most popular recreational activity in America in the 1920s and 1930s," explains Bruce Wigo, president and CEO of the International Swimming Hall of Fame in Fort Lauderdale,

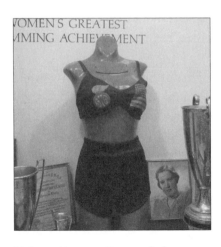

WOMEN'S GREATEST
SWIMMING ACHIEVEMENT

Ederle sewed her own suit, now on display
at the International Swimming Hall of Fame.

Florida. "And the most popular attraction at many amusement parks was the swimming pool." I have traveled here to see what is arguably the best collection of swimming memorabilia in the country. Wigo, whose life-guard looks and wavy blond hair reflect his background as a competitive swimmer and water polo executive, riffles through a box full of old color postcards illustrating outdoor pools and indoor tanks literally swarming with swimmers. "Look at this one—4,000 people a day! And this—2 million gallons of water! They were immense aquatic playgrounds." He eagerly steers me through the exhibits in a two-story shrine to the world of water. It includes medals, images, and detailed accounts of the sport's stars, as well as historic bits of swimming gear: a pair of leather goggles more suitable for a motorcycle than the sea; the corner commemorating Olympian Duke Kahanamoku, complete with Hawaiian shirt and lei; a progression of bathing costumes including Ederle's two-piece silk (with an American flag over the heart) that she wore in the Channel; and a contemporary, cover-all pink burquini.

Wigo's personal passion for swimming is sated during daily swims in the ocean outside his office door, where the water registers a perfect 82 degrees on the day I join him. It is one of many swimming interviews I find myself doing, an unconventional but idyllic setting where your memory has to be really good. Wigo's powerful crawl is an inspiration; his love of the sea palpable. "You jump in the water and feel as if you're in a different world," he explains. "You have no gravity. You put your head under water, and you have no sound. I swim with sea turtles and fish, and every once in a while I see a giant something-or-other swim by. There's something spiritual about it: you get in there, and everything on land disappears. You can think. There's no distractions." Later, over coffee at a nearby restaurant, he elaborates. "This," he says, indicating the canned music in the background, "this is Orwellian. Everywhere there's music. Is it to keep you from thinking?" I ask what he thinks about in the water. "I solve the problems of the world, work and of my family," he says.

One of those problems concerns the other side of the swimming story as it unfolded in the United States.

"Before the Civil War, more blacks than white people swam. But when whites discovered swimming, blacks were totally excluded from safe beaches and America's pools," Wigo says, incensed. "And white culture fought against the integration of swimming pools more than almost any other thing." He reminds me of the ugly incidents and vicious riots during decades of segregation, the laws and the bigotry that kept everyone who wasn't white out of the water. Rather than comply with integration, many pools simply closed.

A movement to build "colored" pools—bluntly advertised in a 1940 "Learn to Swim" poster for the New York City Department of Parks separating dark-skinned swimmers from

How to swim in a divided world

their white peers—was, according to Wigo, "a last-ditch effort to provide 'separate but equal' facilities." It was also too late. "By that time the aquatic culture of the black community had been destroyed." Generations of African Americans grew up with no tradition of swimming. As a result, "the most common black stereotype is, they can't swim. Talk to a black kid on swimming teams. What do his black friends think of him? That he's 'acting white.'"

Several prominent efforts are under way to reverse the trend. Bruce Wigo makes the pitch with his museum, going out of his way to invite African American tourists to see exhibits illustrating the rich history of black swimmers and the many incidents where slaves with fine strokes rescued their nonswimming masters after a shipwreck.

He's also pushing for more public swimming pools to replicate the giant social centers that once captivated Americans. "People built their own pools, in their own backyards or at private clubs, so they wouldn't have to associate with someone they didn't like," he says. And when the public pools closed down, "they were replaced by fifty-meter lap pools, where the sole purpose was to swim competitively. All the social attractions and elements, like slides, restaurants, dance floors and artificial beaches were engineered out of them, thereby ensuring that nonswimmers—code word for minorities—would not find them attractive or inviting. Thus swimming has remained a mostly white activity." Water parks, he says, don't teach people how to swim. He wants the swimming culture to be reborn. Not such a far-fetched image when you recognize that to many, water is sacred. "There's baptism; there's the Greek tomb of the diver," Wigo says. "That's how you pass into the next world. Water is always associated with rebirth."

So we're at it again, reinventing swimming for another age, using a metaphor that is entirely appropriate.

You Know You're a Swimmer If. . . .

- You're crossing a bridge and think, "I could swim across this. . . ."
- People ask you to do a triathlon, and you say you would if it weren't for the run and bike parts.
- You put off the decision to color your hair until after the summer swimming season.
- A hotel/casino in Vegas sends you an email entitled "FLY BACK FREE," and you think they are having some kind of swimming event, only to click on it to see that they are offering to FLY you BACK home FREE.
- You have more swimsuits hanging in your closet than dresses.
- You keep an emergency Swim Bag in your car just in case you pass a pool on the way home.
- You can't remember the last time that you took a shower at home.
- Bugs die of chlorine poisoning when they land on your skin.
- You say to your dog, "Wanna go for a swim?" and she gets more excited than an offering of a walk.
- You find yourself counting strokes instead of sheep to fall asleep at night. Then, just when you're about to fall asleep, instead of your leg twitching a little bit, it does a full whip kick, and you ride the glide to slumberland.
- You get in the water and feel like an eagle in the sky.

—from a series of posts on a US Masters Swimming online forum

3

Fish Out of Water

T HE FIRST FEW *hundred yards are easy. My heart settles in; my body adjusts.
The sea is so sparkly, I feel like a diamond in a glittering field. The goal seems
so tiny, I feel like a ship without radar. But oddly, I feel at home here in the Hellespont.
What, I can't help wondering, might I say if someone were to ask how I'm doing? The
answer, immediately, is both surprising and simple: swimmingly.*

We were fish ourselves hundreds of millions of years ago, awash
in the liquid where life evolved.

"The fish part of us is really very deep, and it's written inside of
the basic structure of our bodies," explains evolutionary biologist
Dr. Neil Shubin of the University of Chicago. He led the team in
2004 that found the missing link between our aquatic ancestors and
land-based mammals—a 375-million-year-old fossil fish that
emerged from the water to breathe air. Its anatomy captures the
transition to future species while reflecting the heritage of its past:
"Our basic structure is actually first seen in fossil fish. They are the
first creatures with skulls like ours. And the genes that make that,

the bits of DNA that build our own body, are actually versions of those seen in building the same body plan in a fish. At some levels we're extremely similar genetically to fish."

I have come to Chicago to meet Dr. Shubin in his anatomy lab, a warren of workbenches and fish models where scholars continue to mine the riches of his discovery. He has filled a critical gap in the evolutionary story and, with the sharp wit and sense of wonder that define our most engaging scientists, has agreed to help me explore the human connection—biologically, evolutionarily—to the water. We begin with the creature he found in the Canadian Arctic, a pioneering voyager from the primordial pool named *Tiktaalik* ("large freshwater fish") in the language of the local Inuit. The model that I see—from just one of many retrieved fossils that range up to nine feet long—is about the length of my arm: a long-bodied, low-finned fish with a placid smile on a face I can only describe as sweet. "Isn't that cute?" Dr. Shubin asks me, clearly pleased with his treasure. "The first thing we saw was the snout. It was upside down, sticking out of the cliff like this," he says, flipping the model and grasping it in his hands.

Beneath *Tiktaalik*'s grin lurked the sharp fangs of a predator on the way to making biological history, a hardy émigré armed with features adapted for life outside the water: a neck that allowed its head to swivel, critical for excursions on land, where you

Fossil of *Tiktaalik roseae*

can't flip your body at will; a flat skull like a crocodile's with eyes on top, the better to see terrestrial prey; lungs that can process air; and articulated bones embedded in its front fins that enabled it to climb out of the past. "Clearly they were able to support their bodies with their fins, like doing a form of a pushup," Dr. Shubin tells me, reaching for a model of the fin and pointing to its stubby little projections. "There's the elbow; there's the wrist. So it functions like a fin—it could paddle around—but it could also support the body. What's really cool are these bones that correspond to ours: this is the radius; this is the ulna; here's the shoulder." The entire fin is about the size of my hand. It is the predecessor of my upper arm and forearm, with distinct joints at the shoulder, elbow, and wrist—all that, in addition to the same gills, scales, and webbing as today's fresh halibut lying on ice chips at my local seafood shop.

Rendering of *Tiktaalik* as it might have moved onto land

In other words, undeniable evidence of what Dr. Shubin calls a "fishapod"—a perfect mix of a fish and a tetrapod, or four-legged land creature. Somewhere along the evolutionary tree, someone with appendages like these veered off onto a limb to help establish everything from dinosaurs to humans.

"You know, every time you bend your head or bend your wrist—and there are other functions as well—these are fish functions that originally appeared in fish living in aquatic ecosystems," he says. In addition, our ears are modified gill bones; a human fetus has gill slits. In sum, "the tool kit that builds our bodies is a version of that which builds a fish."

Which fish?

Dr. Shubin says we humans are closest in terms of anatomy and DNA to lungfish or, lower down what he calls the "tree of cousinness," to sturgeon or paddlefish. Drop further, and it's sharks or shark-like creatures. And way down, the invertebrate predecessor to the fish: the worm. Time to expand the family photo album? "The odds of [*Tiktaalik*] being our exact ancestor are very remote," Shubin writes in his lively and enlightening book, *Your Inner Fish*. "It is more like a cousin of our ancestor." So why don't we talk about our connection to fish? How come we only acknowledge the great apes? "I don't know," he concedes to me. "It's not something that's so obvious to people. Some people have a hard time accepting our relationship to monkeys. Well, it's the worms you need to worry about."

We don't even own the bragging rights to the biggest talent separating us from water dwellers. "Air breathing originally evolved in fish that lived in anoxic waters, waters that were depleted in oxygen," he explains. I think about the brilliantly colored koi slithering around in my fish pond back home: sometimes on hot days, they swim along, reach up, "take a big gulp of air, and come back down," says Shubin, finishing my thought. "Lungs actually are ancient. Air breathing is a fishy thing."

Why it developed—and why the quest for even more air lured *Tiktaalik* and its pals out of their comfort zone in the water back in the late Devonian age—is not clear. Possibly for food, where there were fewer competitors. Possibly to escape prehistoric marine predators. But it wasn't all that they had hoped for: some creatures returned to the water after a time. I ask whether we, today's swimmers, are doing the same.

"In evolutionary terms? No," says Dr. Shubin. "But water is something that is very magical to us. Not because of our anatomy—it's really because of our psyche, the way we see the world. It's the way our brains are wired. Look, I have little kids, and it's hard to pull them out of the pool. We have a natural affinity to water."

Shubin does not accept the Aquatic Ape theory—a tantalizing but controversial hypothesis that humans evolved from a branch of apes who had adapted to life in the water. One claim of evidence: the vestigial webbing that connects our fingers.

"Nobody buys it," he says, speaking for the paleontology community and shaking his head. "Because we really don't have that evidence in our fossil record. It almost makes more sense that we are derived to run on land. That doesn't mean that we're just one-trick horses. We can use those aerobic abilities to swim in water too. I mean, what's great about humans is that we can inhabit almost every environment, right? We're a species that is amazingly variable."

Fish swim because they have to; we do it by choice. Some fish can climb trees and glide through the air; so can we, with proper training and appropriate equipment. And even if our aquatically  rooted anatomy doesn't explain our need to swim, the flexibility we inherited sure makes it easier. For starters, our bodies are mostly made of water which, when you think about it, makes the water we swim in a far less hostile environment. President John F. Kennedy made the connection in a speech about sailing: "All of us have in our veins the exact same percentage of salt in our blood that exists in the ocean, and, therefore, we have salt in our blood, in our sweat, in our tears. We are tied to the ocean. And when we go back to the sea . . . we are going back from whence we came."

Thanks to Archimedes, we understand the principles that make it possible. His Eureka! moment in the bathtub 2,000 years ago in ancient Syracuse may have been apocryphal, but it nonetheless provides a useful illustration of the science that keeps us afloat. All that water spilling over the sides when he lowered himself into the tub revealed the connection between displacement and buoyancy, which is actually a function of density: anything denser than water will sink; less or the same will bob around like a cork. That's us. The human body has almost the same density as water (a ratio that's called specific gravity), a nifty trick of physics that lets us glide on the waves and slide through the surf. Buoyancy makes water a mystical medium: it allows us to weigh less, to feel as if we're flying, to forget about gravity. If it worked on dry land, it would put plastic surgeons out of business; in the water, it is nature's personal swim aid, a no-cost reward for getting wet. And it's enhanced by salt, which is why we float more easily in oceans. When there's an extreme amount—as in the Dead Sea, where salt comprises 35 percent rather than the usual 3 percent—you're so buoyant, you can barely move. The Roman historian Tacitus described the ancient site this way in the second century CE: "These strange waters support what is thrown upon them, as on a solid surface, and all persons, whether they can swim or not, are equally buoyed up by the waves." When I visit the Dead Sea in Israel, my guide puts it more bluntly before I venture in: "As soon as your backside touches the water, you're floating." No kidding. Swimming is impossible; turning on your belly makes you feel like a beetle flipped on its back—your legs pop skyward, unaided, and standing upright is a struggle.

Benjamin Franklin used buoyancy to help conquer fear. "You will be no swimmer till you place some confidence in the power of the water to support you," he advised a nonswimming friend in a letter during the late 1760s. How to do it? In a pond or stream where the water deepens gradually, walk in, up to your chest, and then turn to face the shore. Next, toss a boiled egg into the water—toward the shore—and when it sinks, dive in and try to grab it. "You will find," Dr. Franklin writes, "that the water buoys you up against your inclination; that it is not so easy a thing to sink as you imagined; that you cannot but by active force get down to the egg. Thus you feel the power of the water to support you, and learn to confide in that power; while your endeavours to overcome it and to reach the egg, teach you the manner of acting on the water with your feet and hands."

And then you get to eat the egg.

Buoyancy also lifts the ego when other body parts start to droop. Curvy people float better than lean beans, and women more than men, because even at our slimmest, we have an extra layer of fat distributed throughout our bodies. The scientific term is positive buoyancy, which sounds a lot better than, say, "solid" or "chunky." Wiry guys, and probably some gals, have negative buoyancy, which sounds a lot better than "skinny." Their legs, or entire bodies, go down faster. Most of us are either one or the other. The great long distance swimmer Lynne Cox was born smack in the middle. In her lyrical memoir, *Swimming to Antarctica*, Cox writes about learning that she has "neutral buoyancy. That means," her doctor told her, "your body density is exactly the same as seawater. Your proportion of fat to muscle is perfectly balanced so you don't float or sink in the water; you're at one with the water. We've never seen anything like this before." She meant: in a human. For Cox (whose awesome exploits receive the attention they deserve in Chapter 6), that biological oddity meant "that I didn't have to use energy to either fight against sinking or pull myself down into the water to counteract buoyancy. This enabled me to swim more efficiently."

Effortless in the Dead Sea

Can Giraffes Swim?

It's not the sort of question you can ask a giraffe. And no human has ever reported seeing one take a proper dip. One herd was caught on video wading into the water chest high, but they retreated to shore as the bottom dropped off. The issue isn't size—elephants are graceful swimmers—but shape, which seems to defy the laws of aquatics: up to two tons of bulky mass offset by a flexible tower of a neck, perched atop four formidable legs of two different lengths. Can its lungs, notoriously oversized, hold enough oxygen to enable flotation? Two imaginative paleontologists created a computer model, complete with spots and the little "horns" known as ossicones, and plunked it into the digital drink. Factoring in the effects of drag and density, they found that the giraffe's shorter hind legs would float before its front legs; that in deeper water, it would start to angle downward until its neck rested on or below the surface; that it wouldn't sink but would look "downright uncomfortable." And since it couldn't use its neck to pump up its gait (as it does on land), it likely would be a "very poor" swimmer. Their conclusion: "giraffes can swim, but not at all well."

For ardent giraffe lovers like me, knowing they're landlubbers is just fine. For radio host Peter Sagal, the results are more troubling. "You might wonder who might fund such a study," he mused on NPR's *Wait Wait . . . Don't Tell Me*. "Turns out it was a pack of hyenas."

Understanding the science of our connection to the water is both instructive and reassuring. But that's just the first step. Discovering the effect that water has on our bodies upgrades swimming from a pleasant pastime to a medical must, although the about-face of the medical community since the Middle Ages has led to some, shall we say, exaggerated claims. More than five hundred years ago, Reverend Digby recommended swimming for "purging poisoned humors, drying away contagious diseases, and by this means adding longer date unto the life of man." Time only heightened the hype. A French physician in 1819 said swimming cured everything from masturbation to pulmonary infections to spontaneous dislocation of the femur. Two decades later, a popular handbook called *British Manly Exercises* promised would-be jocks that it was also "useful in . . . the tranquilizing of the nervous system." Around the same time, an American identifying himself only as "An Experienced Swimmer" wrote that swimmers "are not liable to sudden colds, or inflammatory diseases and rarely if ever, suffer from chronic complaints. Their bodies become indurated, their skin is healthy, and all the functions of life are carried on with healthful vigor." A YMCA manual capped it off in 1910 with the claim that swimming outdoors "prevents the growth of gray hair."

If only. Swimmers are hale, not disease-proof; hardy, not ageless. But a century—or five—later, there are alluring indications that regular, vigorous water activity may indeed extend human life. Every time we grind out our laps, we may, in some measure, be swimming in the fountain of youth. The proven benefits read like a wish list from the American Heart Association: swimming can lower blood pressure and optimize cholesterol levels, improve the pumping capacity of the heart and thus enhance circulation, expand the ventilator capacity of the lungs and thus enhance cardiovascular performance. One celebrated study found that mortality rates for swimmers were lower than for those who are sedentary, walkers, and runners.

Cousin *Tiktaalik's* push-ups were just the beginning; swimming is a rhythmic, dynamic activity that uses every large muscle group. It helps build lean muscle mass and promote flexibility. And while it's true that all aerobic exercise leads to many of those results, a recent study shows that swimmers bested joggers and walkers in every cardio number. More significant for a nation with an aging population, you don't hear complaints about bone spurs in the pool. "Swimming is the closest thing on this earth to a perfect sport," writes Dr. Jane Katz, a pioneering swim fitness promoter and educator.

Movie star Esther Williams has often said, "Swimming is the only thing you can do from your first bath to your last without hurting yourself. When you're in the water, you're weightless and ageless."

No knees pounding the pavement. No joints slamming against a ball or a wall. Buoyancy protects the most vulnerable parts of our skeleton. Just ask a pregnant woman. "Suddenly that big bump becomes weightless," rhapsodizes a young mother recalling her blissful Caribbean swims at five months along.

For people with certain disabilities swimming feels like a miracle. Byron was born with a club foot, a contracted Achilles tendon that gave him a pronounced and debilitating limp. In the water, he moved like an eel. "I can keep myself up for hours in the sea," he wrote. "I delight in it, and come out with a buoyancy of spirits I never feel on any other occasion. If I believed in . . . transmigration . . . I should think I had been made a Merman in some former state of existence." Annette Kellerman, the Australian swimmer who helped usher American women into the water with well-publicized endurance swims and sexy films, wore heavy iron braces on her legs as a child, the result of some sort of bone ailment. Swimming lessons turned her into a mermaid.

I started swimming in earnest after recovering from a broken kneecap in 1977, when eight weeks in a full-leg cast left my joint immobile and my quadriceps withered. Regular laps helped restore both muscle and flexibility. Since then, I've expanded my workouts to the rest of my body, adding weight training and Pilates in a weekly regime. I was in reasonably good shape before I began my Hellespont training. But the water upped the ante.

"Swimmers Really Do Report 'Feeling Better,'" reads the headline over one study of mood changes, an indication of how swimming can also promote mental health, or at least a sense of well-being. Kellerman, who spent much of her life promoting her own healthful lifestyle, put it in terms that might get her elected today: "For the woman who swelters in her kitchen or lolls in a drawing room, for the man who sits half his life in an office chair, an occasional swim does as much good as six months' vacation. That weary feeling goes away for once in the cool, quiet water. Tired men and tired women forget that stocks and cakes have fallen."

Or as a swimming instructor from another era declared, "The experienced swimmer when in the water may be classed among the happiest of mortals in the happiest of moods, and in the most complete enjoyment of the most delightful of exercises." I think that's partly biological: our skin is our largest organ, so swimming is our most sensuous sport. And partly revolutionary. Swimming, says Kellerman, "is the one sport in which women are not at a disadvantage with the stronger sex. And I feel that I have a right to speak thus for I know that the sea has brought me from a little lame child to the woman I am to-day."

Alas, this otherwise ideal sport may not do much for our waistlines. While swimming can smooth out the figure and certainly burn

Health

Of exercises, swimming's best,
  Strengthens the muscles and the chest,
  And all their fleshy parts confirms.
 Extends, and stretches legs and arms,
And, with a nimble retro-spring,
Contracts, and brings them back again.
As 'tis the best, so 'tis the sum
Of exercises all in one,
And of all motions most compleat,
Because 'tis vi'lent without heat.

—Dr. Edward Baynard, from his poem "Health," 1764

fat, it does not directly promote weight loss. According to Dr. Joel Stager, associate director of Indiana University's Department of Kinesiology, that's because "losing weight is about efficiency—the amount of work done divided by the metabolic cost of doing that work." The problem, he tells me, "is that most people who need to lose weight are so out of shape, they can't swim far enough to make a difference. And the better swimmer you are, the less metabolic work you're doing. So as you become more efficient, if you're swimming to lose weight, you are defeating your purpose by getting better." Blame it, he says, on buoyancy, which "reduces the energy expenditure associated with swimming." It's a dilemma, but not one that troubles Dr. Stager. Weight, he points out, is not a good index, especially since muscle mass weighs more than fat.

We are talking at his office at IU's main Bloomington campus, a lush, leafy enclave of gentle hills and imposing limestone buildings that could be the movie set for Collegetown, U.S.A. Dr. Stager, who is also director of the Counsilman Center for the Science of Swimming, is a principal investigator of an ambitious study on the health effects of swimming on the human body, focusing on longtime members of US Masters Swimming, a national organization of more than 50,000 adults who want to stay fit in the water. USMS clubs are all over the country, offering everything from tune-ups to killer workouts to international competitions. I joined in January 2011 to get ready for my personal marathon, hoping the regular drills and connection with other swimmers might crank up my strokes and speed to Hellespont level. I have also agreed to take part in Dr. Stager's study. The Counsilman Center, headquartered in the giant Health, Physical Education and Recreation building (or HPER, known appropriately on this go-go campus as Hyper), is named for James E. (Doc) Counsilman, the celebrated coach who led Indiana's male swimmers and divers to dozens of titles. He also coached Mark Spitz, the Olympic swimming world's first seven-medal man. A world record breaststroker, Counsilman became the oldest person to swim the English Channel in 1979, at the age of fifty-eight (a record since broken), which he did "to challenge himself," says Stager. He died in 2004 from Parkinson's disease.

Counsilman's legendary innovations at the Bloomington pool that anchors this complex—like the wall-mounted pace clocks (one is still there), so that athletes could monitor their own time—made him the authority of his day, a giant in the field who was proudest, according to Joel Stager, "of bringing science and sport together." His breakthrough book, *The Science of Swimming*, published in 1968, became the swim coaching bible. His forte was technique. Dr. Stager's interest is exercise physiology—the heart-lung-muscle triad. "What floats my boat is, how does Michael Phelps accomplish it?" he explains. And the $64,000 corollary: Does swimming keep you young? At fifty-nine, Joel Stager is his own best advertisement, with the streamlined body and boyish good looks of the competitive swimmer that he was when he first came to work with Counsilman in the mid-1970s. He loves the sport and swims daily in the pool just below his office—3,000 yards every noon, five days a week—a rigorous workout in Doc's old pool with like-minded fanatics who leave me panting in their wake. At IU, everyone I meet swims. Very, very well.

"You can come up with an excuse every day why not to get into the water," says Dr. Stager, a sprinter. "I am proud that I set an example for my students. This is what we profess, but it's also what we do." Stager's students are equally committed swim groupies, putting swimming through the microscope of a series of investigations. One is researching the thermoregulation of water versus air; another, the energy value of chocolate milk for racers. I hear about a "start study," examining how swimmers go off the blocks; about research on swimmers' hands: Is there an ideal size? In a world that rewards victory-by-a-fingernail, these are not frivolous topics. And the students—broad-shouldered and muscular, padding about in flip-flops—fully appreciate the opportunity to study the sport that sustains them. "It's about being in the water; it's meditation," says a well-built graduate student in a black tee revealing killer biceps. "I've come up with some research thoughts doing laps. You learn a lot about life by swimming."

What Joel Stager is learning may change our understanding of the human body—in particular, the central nervous system. "Our hypothesis is that maintenance of physical activity—specifically swimming—preserves higher brain activity," he says. "And then some." His project, in conjunction with the IU Brain Science Lab, focuses on the hard-swimming members of US Masters: men and women who swim 3,500 to 5,000 yards (that's two to three miles) three to five times a week. Some have been doing it for nearly twenty years. "There are," Stager says, "few comparable populations who engage in routine intensive daily exercise for decades."

That's a bit above my fitness grade, but for the sake of the study, I'm one of them, with a good opportunity to see where I fit into the swimming world. After my vitals are recorded, my heart rate is monitored as I fast-walk around the indoor track. I am checked for motor control and balance on a treadmill, then hooked up to electrodes to test my nerve conduction velocity, as a weak electrical current tickles my funny bone. I opt out of the brain MRI because there's a pin in my kneecap, a result of the break that got me swimming in the first place. But I get totally into the cognitive ability tests to check my memory, reasoning, logical thought, perceptual speed, and nonverbal learning. I am asked to count backwards by threes and recall sets of scrambled letters, I have to rearrange letters and numbers read to me out of order, I manipulate symbols and numbers and identify missing pieces for spatial recognition, and somewhere I seem to recall a light box where I had to put certain cards in place. After two days of tests, and another week at home recording my activities in a diary, my part in the study is over. How'd I do?

"All is well!" reports Colleen McCracken, the PhD candidate who is running the study. "Your cognitive results placed you in the top quartile," she says, meaning that my brain is clicking along just fine. Phew. And "your arteries can relax and contract better than [those of] most people your age," she says, meaning that my cardio system is pumping away happily. Double phew. I still need to improve my oxygen consumption—to get my endurance up—and while my body mass index is normal and healthy for the general population, other Masters Swimmers are leaner and meaner. Didn't need a test for that one. But overall, it's good news: swimming may be keeping me healthy. And I have contributed to something that may change the way we think about it.

"Yes, swimming is good for your heart," Dr. Stager tells me. "We've found that the arteries of older USMS members tend to be more elastic than those of younger nonswimmers. And that the muscle mass of older Masters Swimmers is equivalent to [that in] persons fifteen years younger. Masters Swimmers have lower average heart rates than sedentary controls. That's good. But it also appears to be good for your brain." Among the findings so far: Active swimmers appear to have greater cell density and "connectedness" in the cerebellum, which could mean protection from age-related complications in gait and balance that lead to falls. And they show very little decline in nerve conduction velocity (NCV)—the speed with

Word cloud produced from responses to a question posed by *Swimmer* magazine: "What adjective best describes swimming?"

which your brain tells your muscles what to do: the NCV rate in eighty-year-old swimmers was similar to that of fifty-year-olds in the general population. Smaller age-related declines have also been found in Masters Swimmers' working memory capacity, which is reflected in decision making and reaction time in making decisions.

I ask if he believes that the evidence so far is incontrovertible that swimming slows down the aging process.

"Yes," Dr. Stager says, "but we have to be careful with the terminology. Maybe typical lifestyles—sedentary lifestyles—accelerate what we commonly think of as aging. What we're really trying to do is separate sedentarism from aging. So what we're saying is, the Masters Swimmers—and this is a flip—demonstrate what is necessarily aging. What the general population is demonstrating is sedentarism."

In other words, maybe Masters Swimmers are the norm; they're how we should all look. And they are aging less quickly than the rest of the population.

"Absolutely," he says. "What we used to think was a necessary consequence of aging now appears to be more related to lifestyle choices. This is really important."

It is a striking preliminary conclusion for a work still in progress, and Joel Stager says the message is simple: "One more incentive to get in the water."

4

Different Strokes. . . .

I AM SWIMMING *upstream without a paddle. Yes, other humans are in the Hellespont with me, but they're nowhere near, and yes, there are safety boats just in case, but that would be cheating. Stroke after stroke it's just me in the sea, using arms and legs and abs (oh, that critical core) to cut through the current toward the other shore. Swimming is the ultimate on-your-own activity. Everyone else gets stuff to make it easier: skis, skates, bats, wheels, sticks, gloves, racquets, slick shoes. Even teammates to help reach the goal. Not us. An equipment malfunction in swimming means some part of your body has broken down. My favorite passage from an early Greek poem about this crossing describes Leander this way: "Himself the crew, the cargo and the ship." Translation: no flippers, no noodles, no rope lines to hang on to. You do it yourself, as I am right now, and the way you do it in swimming is called strokes.*

"Lynn, relax your shoulders! Lynn, stretch even further with those lovely long arms!" "Lynn, get your head deeper into the water, like this!" Fiona Southwell, the eternally upbeat, utterly tireless British Channel swimmer, gave me some pointers the day before this event, at a beachside clinic designed to make the waters of the Hellespont

less terrifying. For half an hour I was directed to swim all the way out to one buoy and then circle back, letting my body get used to the currents and the surprisingly salty taste. The orientation worked: I am comfortable now in this foreign sea, reaching for the other side with previously untapped energy. But the other side is so far away! To get there, I'm swimming freestyle, the better to pierce the oncoming tide. Every now and then I slide into a breaststroke, my rest stroke, to catch my breath and sight the route. Am I going in the right direction? Has the course zigged while I zagged? How did Byron find the Asian shore two hundred years ago without the radio tower that I'm locked onto? Once in a while I flip over onto my back for a complete change of pace—to inhale at will, to stretch my shoulders, to gaze at the perfect blue sky and the European hills I've left behind. It's also a chance to dream. How cool is it to swim from Europe to Asia? How cool am I? Could I do this twice a day and make passionate love in between?

"The definition of swimming," according to one nineteenth-century instructor, is "to keep yourself afloat and make progress. It matters little how this is done—in what mode or form—as long as it is done." Simple enough. Sir Isaac Newton made it simpler: "To every action there is an equal and opposite reaction." That's his Third Law of Motion, which is really the first law of swimming: to get anywhere in the water you must either pull it toward you or push it away. It will reciprocate by sending you in the opposite direction. In the language of swimming, pulling or pushing is the "catch"; returning your arm or leg to the starting point is "recovery." The alternative to both is floating motionless (see the previous chapter on buoyancy), a perfectly pleasant sensation that, depending on the current, either reroutes your journey or contributes little to it, whether your goal is the other side of an ancient channel, the end of the pool, or the wooden raft in the lake. In other words, you need to move, a detail that seems to have eluded the otherwise exacting Romantic poet Percy Bysshe Shelley. One day in Italy he is said to have lamented, "Why can't I swim, it seems so very easy?" When his friend the biographer Edward John Trelawny said, "Because you think you can't," Shelley plunged into the Arno River and dropped like a rock until Trelawny retrieved him.

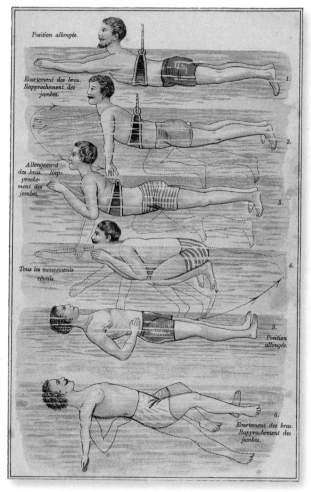

How to swim, French style, 1900

It takes more than just physics and will power to move through a medium some eight hundred times denser than air—where you are horizontal, where you need to move all four limbs at once in an environment without gravity (which means nothing to stand on or push off against), and where you can't always breathe when you want to. It is "the most difficult art there is," pronounced Ralph Thomas, an accomplished swimmer so convinced of its value to humankind, he catalogued every known book in print about it at the end of the nineteenth century. "To swim badly, as to do anything badly, is perfectly easy," he went on. "But to move about, on or under the water with ease and without apparent effort, quietly and without splashing, requires much diligent practice." And while the goal may be to slip through liquid as fluently as a fish, the modern development of human swimming strokes actually owes more to the frog, the dog, the dolphin, and the butterfly.

We begin with the frog, the accomplished little amphibian whose name was appropriated for the leg action of the breaststroke, "the first degree of Swimming," in Reverend Digby's pioneering manual. It was also known as the "human" stroke or the "chest stroke," because you swim on your belly with your head facing comfortably forward. For more than three hundred years, the breaststroke was effectively the only way Europeans and Americans swam across any body of water. It's how Ben Franklin stroked down the Thames, how Byron crossed the Hellespont, how Webb made it across the English Channel (although the then-prevalent technique of keeping his head out of the water for twenty-one hours left him with painful blisters on the back of his neck; he also moved his arms and legs simultaneously). The fundamentals were recognizable: sweep out and back with the arms, then snap them forward; draw the legs up and out, then back. Whoosh! You bolt ahead in the water. For several centuries, pupils were advised to learn it by consulting the acknowledged expert. "For the leg stroke there is no better model than a frog, whose action in swimming should be copied exactly," advised one author. The frog was "the only correct master," according to another. The authoritative *Encyclopedia Britannica* of 1797 quoted "very expert swimmers" as recommending "that some frogs be kept in a tub of water as examples" to would-be swimmers.

Breaststroke

I made the discovery on my own—spending hours as a toddler by a lake in Pennsylvania's Pocono Mountains watching long, rubbery frog limbs flex up and out and back again. Hanging out with the little green guys gave me a leg up on learning, and I developed my own forceful frog kick that serves me well today. I could breaststroke forever. But the image of a small amphibian imprisoned in a basin to educate a grown human was irresistible to Restoration playwright Thomas Shadwell. In *The Virtuoso* (widely seen as a satire on the science of the day) he ridiculed what must have been a very common dryland occurrence. The scene is described by Lady Gimcrack as her husband learns to swim: "He has a frog in a bowl of water, tied with a packthread by the loins; which packthread Sir Nicholas holds in his teeth, lying upon his belly on a table; and as the frog strikes, he strikes; and his swimming-master stands by, to tell him when he does well or ill." Later we come upon Sir Nicholas himself, lying on the table mid–frog-kick. He is asked if he has ever tried out the stroke in the water. "No, sir," he replies, "but I swim most exquisitely on land. . . . I hate the water. . . . I content myself with the speculative part of swimming."

For the latter part of his argument, I defer to my hero, suffrage leader Susan B. Anthony, who as far as I know never swam a day in her life but still understood the urgency of confronting it, like everything else, on its home territory: "Women can't swim as a rule," she said in 1883, referring less to the breaststroke or any other stroke

Mechanical swimming teacher
from Germany

than to women's second-class status in society, "and never will be able to do so—unless thrown into the water to learn the art."

Which didn't stop a host of enterprising inventors from dreaming up some eccentric, if not tortuous, contraptions to save would-be swimmers from the inconvenience of getting wet. They ranged from simple chest slings to hoist the pupil into midair (the better to move his arms and legs around), to complicated platforms with jointed limb rests at the corners, and a rubber air bag supported by a metal framework devised by a Scotsman named John S. Levett. His invention, wrote a (legitimate) swim instructor, "had its recommendations, but as poor Levett was himself drowned a year later on, when exhibiting the apparatus in the sea at Blackpool, no one took any further interest." Understandably so.

Other inventors ginned up gadgets to aid the already waterborne: corks strung together in belts; gloves and boots with duck-like webbing that spread out like an umbrella; flexible tails to support the tailless.

Fortunately, swim instruction soon focused on the stroke, not the stroke aid. And the breaststroke itself changed: instead of executing arms and legs together, it turned out that you got further ahead by staggering the motions. And putting your face in the water allowed for a nice, long, energy-saving glide. In that way, the breaststroke remained "the ordinary and most straightforward style of swimming," someone proclaimed. It is "and will always be, the most popular."

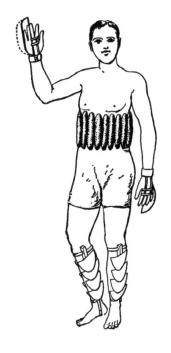

How to swim without wasting energy: cork belt, hand paddles, extending shin flaps—all "ridiculous," said one contemporary.

Turn the breaststroke on its side, keep the bottom arm stretched out, and you get the sidestroke, which was early promoted for its speed and economy: "one side may rest, while the other is employed."

Also known as side swimming, or the underarm stroke, it had become the racing stroke of choice in London by the mid-nineteenth century. "It is," pronounced journalist Robert Patrick Watson, "the most beautiful and the most graceful means of transit through the water." And

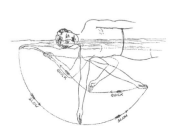

Sidestroke

one of the easiest to learn. Mastering the stroke at the age of forty after splashing helplessly about was a revelation to one writer: "All at once I knew how a fish would feel if it could suddenly walk." In time the kick shifted slightly from frog-like to scissors-like, and swifter swimmers figured out that raising the stroking arm out of the water rather than pushing through it during recovery was even more effective. Thus was born the overhand sidestroke, aka the English sidestroke, or just the overhand, the ultimate lung buster for several generations. It is, reported one contemporary, "most exhausting, and always involves a great expenditure of strength; it is only used where rapidity is needed for a short distance to speed."

The backstroke wasn't so much invented as described, recommended as the "most easy" to a world emerging from the Dark Ages. At first it was legs only—in an upside-down (here we go again) frog kick, arms resting on the belly. But humans have usable arms as well, so they were added in a sculling motion, then an inverted breast stroke sweep, and finally with the one-at-a-time reach and pull that is also called the back crawl. When the legs switched to what we now call the flutter kick, the stroke was complete—but not an instant success. The swim master at England's Eton College called it a "waste of time . . . useless." Another coach dismissed it as too slow for competition, which would surely be a surprise to world record holder Aaron Piersol, who whipped through four lengths of an Olympic pool in less time than it takes to boil water.

The major problem with being on your back is that you can't see where you're going, which may be why the belly-down breaststroke and the more breathable side stroke reigned so long. But they too yielded to progress, as the motion of both legs and arms switched from sweeps and thrusts to pulls and beats—and the brief appearance of the dog in swimming history. Watch Lassie when she gets in the

"Please, Al. You know the backstroke scares the children."

water, and you immediately recognize the doggy paddle, or dog stroke. "Think not this way hard," advised Renaissance chroniclers, "for many ignorantly fall upon this kind of Swimming . . . and are able to bear themselves up so in high water, before ever they learn't to swim." That apparent contradiction is easily understood by anyone watching a beginner or small children in the water; often the first primitive movements pre—swim school are these, which Australian swimming champion Charles Steedman called "the crawl," no doubt because the paddler seemed to be creeping across the water. The term was not then well known; in fact, his 1867 book may be the first time the word "crawl" was used in swimming literature. It would soon have a far different meaning.

Crawl, or freestyle

The novelty of the "hand-over-hand" stroke (also called "the thrust") was notably observed by artist George Catlin on his travels through the unexplored American West. He was so taken by the way the Mandan Indians swam—"quite different from . . . the usual mode of swimming, in the polished world"—he faithfully described their stroke in the journals he published in London in 1844:

> The Indian, instead of parting his hands simultaneously under the chin, and making the stroke outward, in a horizontal direction, causing thereby a serious strain upon the chest, throws his body alternately upon the left and the right side, raising one arm entirely above the water and reaching as far forward as he can, to dip it, whilst his whole weight and force are spent upon the one that is passing under him, and like a paddle propelling him along; whilst this arm is making a half circle, and is being raised out of the water behind him, the opposite arm is describing a similar arch in the air over his head, to be dipped in the water as far as he can reach before him, with the hand turned under, forming a sort of bucket, to act most effectively as it passes in its turn underneath him.

That enticing description likely sparked the British Swimming Society's invitation to a group of Ojibwa Indians later that year. The Native Americans had been ferried across the Atlantic by Canadian entrepreneur Arthur Rankin as a touring exhibit for a British public spellbound by the "noble savages." Coincidentally, Catlin then enlisted them to promote his own exhibition of portraits and Indian artifacts at Piccadilly's famed Egyptian Hall—part of a living display (with salary). They even performed a war dance for Queen Victoria at Windsor Castle. The Swimming Society cooked up a race, promising a medal (first-class, silver) for the fastest Indian. So at high noon one April day in 1844, a party of Ojibwa, in full regalia and on horse-back, arrived by what must have been an unusually large omnibus to an eager crowd at the High Holborn baths. With the water temperature cranked up to 85 degrees (at the request of the Indians' medical advisor), the competitors—Wenishkaweabee, or Flying Gull, and Sahma, or Tobacco—removed their costumes, lined up, and dived in.

The only surviving report of the performance does not specify how far they stripped down, but since the Indian women who had accompanied them were immediately relegated to another room, it's likely that the visitors swam unclothed. At a signal they were off, completing 130 feet, almost an Olympic length, in less than thirty seconds. Flying Gull won by more than a body length. They repeated the race back to the start, and Flying Gull again edged out Tobacco. Today, that pace wouldn't even qualify for bronze; it's about ten sec-onds slower than the world record. And later the Indians were handily defeated by English breaststroking champion Harold Kenworthy. But what wowed the witnesses and the unnamed sports reporter for the *London Times* was not so much their speed as their technique: "Their style of swimming is totally un-European," he wrote. "They lash the water violently with their arms, like the sails of a windmill, and beat downwards with their feet, blowing with force, and forming grotesque antics." It was nothing like the breaststroke.

Curiously, the unusual new practice died in the waters of High Holborn, at least temporarily. After a celebratory toast with wine and biscuits, the Ojibwas returned to their jobs at Catlin's gallery. Flying Gull's silver medal was promised within the week. But the image of his flying arms was indelible. Almost thirty years later, a twenty-one-year-old Englishman named John Trudgen (occasionally spelled Trudgeon) won a race that dazzled eyewitnesses and revived old memories. He "swam with both arms entirely out of the water, an action peculiar to Indians," announced the editor of the *Swimming Record* in 1873. "Both arms are thrown partly sideways, but very slovenly, and the head kept completely above water." Trudgen said he'd learned the stroke from native tribes in Argentina. But unlike his Ojibwa predecessors, "his time was very fast"—so fast that he "degenerated Londoners to the level of mediocrity." So fast that John Trudgen's name was attached to the hot new stroke.

While speedy, the stroke looked stilted. With the head always up and the legs imitating the frog, not the flutter, the swimmer surged ahead with a herky-jerky motion. "The body is lifted at each stroke," noted one observer, "and at each swing of the arms seems to be hurled forward, a considerable swirl of the water occurring as each movement is finished." Like *Tiktaalik* the Trudgen was a stroke in transition, evolving from the sea of the breaststroke to a new world of accomplishment. Gradually it morphed into a narrower, more streamlined version, with the head almost fully immersed and the legs more scissors than frog as the body rolled side to the side. It was, to some, "the king of all strokes . . . the fastest of all those which there is any fun in swimming. It is the one stroke which gives the highest speed with the least exertion: it is the one stroke which is suited equally for speed and distance, for racing and pleasure, for the swimming-tank and the open sea."

But it wasn't soup yet. There are conflicting accounts about the next enhancement. Either:

In 1902, fifteen-year-old Dick Cavill, an Australian member of a prominent swimming family, sped to victory in a hundred-yard race combining the top half of the Trudgen, that is, the alternating overarm movements, with a new leg motion. One look at the elaborate description confirms how new: the legs were "kicked down from the knee to the toe on to the surface by the feet being alternately raised out of the water, and without the body being turned from side to side." We call it the flutter kick. Cavill claimed that he'd seen it on a racer who'd learned it from natives in the Solomon Islands. As for the stroke itself, "the swimmer appears to be crawling over the water instead of being in it."

Or:

When Alick Wickham, the racer who'd learned it in the Solomons, used it in a race, a Sydney coach said, "Look at that kid crawling."

Or:

When Cavill did it, opponents said he "was crawling all over me."

Whichever, it was called the Trudgen crawl or, after its first performer, Australian crawl. By the time American racers adopted it, the so-called two-beat kick (one per arm stroke) changed to six (three per arm). Another Australian figured out that breathing in sync with the strokes made it even more efficient. The crawl as we know it was set, "the newest and the fastest," a physics teacher wrote in 1910, "of all swimming-strokes."

It would continue to be streamlined. And confusing. I was taught the Trudgen crawl with both a flutter kick and a scissors kick, alternating with each arm. This is not an exact science.

Even the reliable breaststroke was rearranged yet again when someone wanted to get to the wall more quickly. Several different swimmers in the 1930s are credited with abandoning the underwater sweep of the arms to bring them up and out of the water, then combining that motion with an undulating kick: the butterfly. Such a delicate-sounding name for such a pain-producing stroke, though one of the most splendid to watch when it's done well. It took another few decades for the swimming world to accept the new leg stroke, the maddeningly difficult movement that is named for the affable dolphin. The fly, as it's known, is the ultimate test of flexibility and core strength, the toughest stroke to execute well. While your core is undulating and your feet are flexing, your arms are circling

Breaststroke

"Swimming-strokes are like clothes," observed one instructor. "One does not get on comfortably with only one suit." Comedian and writer Laurie Kilmartin, a former competitive breaststroker, describes the styles in her own swimming wardrobe:

Freestyle: Truly a dull and unimaginative stroke. Left arm, right arm, left kick, right kick. What kind of person finds intellectual stimulation in this sort of repetition? Clomp, clomp, clomp. Freestyle is an elephant's stroke, all apologies to elephants. It is a stroke for people who stop at yellow lights and excel at algebra. Freestylers prefer Windows to Macintosh, Kenny G to Miles Davis and day to night.

Backstroke: Do you not realize that you are upside down?

Butterfly: Good Lord. When will this most violent of strokes be committed to an insane asylum? The loud uncle of swimming, butterfly boorishly hogs the remote control, making all the other strokes watch football on Thanksgiving Day. Grow up. You are making a scene.

Breaststroke: Breaststroke is all that is noble and good in this cruel world. Many deities . . . enjoy the solitude of this most subtle of strokes. Breaststroke has refined tastes. It reads the *New Yorker* and paints abstracts with oil. Breaststroke, we suspect, enjoys a martini now and again. (Contrast this with the alcoholic butterfly, which pounds Budweisers from cans, shoplifted from a 7–11). It soothes the inner beast and acts as a gentle tonic on a troubled heart. Breaststroke, you see, is in harmony with the universe; its pull and kick chase one another in playful symmetry. And if that weren't enough, breaststroke also boasts the crown jewel of competitive swimming, the pulldown . . . a holy moment of shrouded watery silence. Breaststrokers go to chapel during the pulldown (often giving thanks that they are not backstrokers), and break to the surface only when their brave lungs are nearly burst. . . . Breaststroke is Yin and Yang, Rum and Coke . . .

Join us.

almost 360 degrees, in the middle of which you have to breathe. It is beyond irony that nature's butterfly cannot swim.

Today there are four official competitive swim strokes: fly, back, breast, and freestyle. I'm working hardest on the last, because you can never get good enough at the crawl. But my heart still belongs to the breaststroke. Sigmund Freud reportedly liked it because it kept his beard dry. Works for the hair on the top of your head as well. Laura Hamel, editor of *Swimmer* magazine and a breaststroker, calls it "the thinking person's stroke. Look at the rule book," she tells me, pointing out that defining the breaststroke takes up more space than any other. "It's so difficult to judge." A more romantic breaststroker compares its up-and-down rhythm to the sun and moon "rising and falling around the horizon each day." A poet sees the coming together of the hands as prayer. You can see when you breaststroke. You can breathe. You can think when you glide. I'm just saying.

"Lynn, get your legs up!"

"Lynn, use your core!"

"Lynn, use your triceps, not your forearm!"

That's just some of what I've been told since I decided to ratchet up my freestyle to a new level—a proficiency that could, among other things, get me across the Hellespont. Truth is, I'd always thought of myself as a perfectly elegant mermaid, slipping through the ripples, or waves, of any blue box or ocean I happened to inhabit. Not until I got into the pool at my twice-weekly Masters drills did I realize I might be behind the curve. It has been humbling.

I had to learn lap etiquette (swim counterclockwise, leaving space behind the leader; tap gently on someone's foot if you want to pass) and new lingo ("Okay, we're going to do five by two hundred free pull at 3:15, breathing five, seven, seven, five for each two hundred"—huh?). I reacquainted myself with a kickboard, welcomed the ease of swimming with the little Styrofoam wedge called the "pull buoy" that fits between your thighs and floats your legs so you can work on your arms, and agonized over the sequence of sprints that squeezed every bit of air out of my lungs. I also had to retrain my limbs, trying to erase the muscle memory of many decades, to come up to speed.

The experts call it "a feel for the water"—the heightened focus that makes gifted swimmers aware of every ripple across each of those "itty bitty muscles that you don't use for anything else in your life," explains champion Olympic backstroker Natalie Coughlin. "You have to know what your belly is doing while also knowing what your shins and your feet and your arms are doing." It's a mental exercise, she tells me, "knowing the sensation of the water. And if you don't do it all the time, you start to lose it."

Especially when the rules have changed. For example: When I was taught the crawl as a toddler, you swam flat, flat as a flounder. And if you asked the instructor to demonstrate on dry land, he or she would stand still and move only the arms. Right, left, right left. Ditto about breathing: we were taught to fill our lungs by turning the head—not the whole body. Today it's about the roll: keeping the head and spine in a line and making the body more knife than pancake when you reach forward. And when you ask someone to show you how, they stand on deck and do this kind of jitterbuggy dance thing that moves the hips and the opposite arm, back and forth. "You have to learn to line everything up, sort of like Pilates in the water," advises George Block, a celebrated former club coach from San Antonio, Texas, who has been recommended to me as a really good explainer. "Use your core to streamline and then the arms and legs to apply propulsion."

I am talking to him by telephone, but he is so graphic, you can probably learn from your living room. "Our bodies are a balloon— your lungs a giant airbag—tied to an anchor, your legs," he says. "Your legs are your biggest muscles, and they're farthest from the heart. So they're just air suckers. They cost a lot of oxygen and a lot of heartbeats to propel you. You need muscle strength, but it's more neurological than physiological, because you have to learn to recruit the right muscles. And the right muscles in swimming are all small. It's a real pulsating sport. Everything is slow-fast, slow-fast, whatever movement you're making. In freestyle: first you have to flex your wrist, your fingers go down, your palms start to face back, and then your elbow rotates. You get your whole forearm facing back, trying to create this big paddle up front. And you want that to be relatively slow. Can you feel the water? Can you get hold of it, as it wraps around your forearm? And then you want to kick in your big muscles of your lats and your triceps. And phoom! Shoot it back as fast and as far as you can. So the whole stroke accelerates from slow at the beginning to fast at the end."

And the legs? "The legs are pretty constant, almost like a metronome going against an upper body movement that's going from slow to fast. So it's almost like having a percussion section or a string section doing one thing where your wind instruments are playing something different."

I am reminded of what another coach told me as I practiced in the pool: "You have to learn to walk and chew gum at the same time." George Block agrees. "Yes. And it's really confusing to tell kids to do it and then to relax while doing it! And to keep their elbows up underwater."

It's about weight shifts, subtle movement, making the water work for you. And it's a lot to take in, but it makes sense when you get it right, as I find myself doing roughly once an hour. I worried that swimming would become work, not fun—that the pleasure of being in the water would turn into drudgery. Not a chance. Too much to learn.

Dr. Jane Katz, the New York expert, gives me more specific tips when she kindly agrees to swim with me one morning: Extend my arm further forward on each stroke, she says; roll slightly to the nonbreathing side (head down in the water) to keep from being flat, to slice through the water better; kick my legs only twice on each stroke to keep from getting breathless. Rely on my arms. "Yes, it will tire you out as you learn," she acknowledges, nimbly hoisting herself out of the pool after my lesson. "But do it gradually—half a lap, then a whole lap, then as you just swim along. It will come." She's right—I feel more agile and am swimming better.

This is how many swimmers learn and improve—focusing on different limbs and muscles, then knitting them together over time. Terry Laughlin uses a different system, one that's helped a lot of

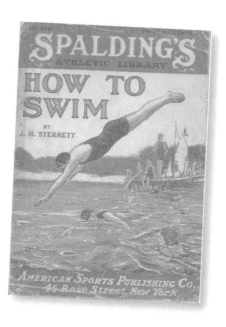

adults get into the water for the first time. It's called Total Immersion, and it emphasizes balance, not body parts. "It's not about an 'arms department' and a 'legs department,'" he tells me. "It's about whole-body streamlining. Learn how your body naturally behaves in the water." Laughlin, whose everyman shape at sixty belies a sleek crawl, demonstrates his technique when I drive up to visit him in New Paltz, New York, a quiet community in the Hudson River valley nearly two hours north of Manhattan. The warmth of his basement pool is a welcome respite from the snow on the wintry ground—it's an Endless Pool, one of those bigger-than-a-bathtub tanks with a controllable current that streams by at a soothing 89 degrees. "Pay attention to the water flowing cleanly around you," Laughlin says, sliding in for the lessons.

With the help of a video camera, he analyzes my problem immediately: I'm not efficient in the water. "You see what your arms and legs are doing," he explains, after showing me myself on the tape. "What you think is propelling is mostly stabilizing. Correcting your body position. You're moving water around rather than moving through it." The main message: use your gut for balance; streamline your body; soften your limbs. "Stop thinking about using your arm muscles to push on the water molecules behind you," he says, showing me the unnecessary force that I'm employing. "Use them to separate the water molecules in front of you. You still use it to push back, but that's secondary to what I call a human-sized sleeve through which you slip the rest of your body. Try to be gentle and light and gather moonbeams." It is indeed a different approach: less power, more balance. I understand why Terry Laughlin is the talk of the internet, with followers from around the globe. The day I'm there, a middle-aged Canadian, who looks more like a wrestler than a swimmer, has flown from his home just below the Arctic Circle to Montreal, and then driven four hours for his lesson, to keep up with his young son. "Terry helped me to feel the water," he tells me, "the way I felt the air as a kid when I put my hand out the window of a moving car. I practice each move fifty times when I'm done."

Many months later, when the snow has melted and the summer sun allows long plunges into the water, I emerge from a mile workout through the bay off New York's Long Island to find myself chatting with a fellow from Ohio who has admired my stroke. "I'm a relatively new swimmer," he says, "trying to do the same. I've read this book called *Total Immersion*, and I've been getting the lessons online." When I tell him I know Terry Laughlin, his eyes widen as if I've mentioned a rock star.

Not everyone is a *TI* fan. Some racing coaches question his downgrading of power, his dismissal of proven techniques—he calls pull buoys and kickboards and flippers "contaminants" because they teach separation rather than integration of body parts. Laughlin himself regrets some of what he published in his first book and has prepared a revised edition. But his principles seem practical, similar to everything else I've learned, just packaged slightly differently. I find myself incorporating much of it into my Masters drills. In fact, all the advice I've gotten is helpful—now I just need to apply it, to sort through all the things I've learned and figure out which ones work for me.

"There's no one way to swim," says Russell Mark, a scientist and performance expert with USA Swimming. "A lot of it depends on body type, range of motion, flexibility, strength, the length of your arms and legs. A lot of our best swimmers are just so natural in the water, they make it look so easy. And a lot of recreational swimmers have to work to stay on top of the water. With beginners I want to say, 'Hey, just relax. You don't have to fight the water.'"

It's partly the art of surrender, following your senses rather than your brain. Some also call it *being* the stroke, *being* the pool or the ocean. It is, they say, the Zen of swimming. And it's where the very best swimmers live—both physically and emotionally. When I ask Michael Phelps if being in the water is a good feeling, he answers without hesitation: "It's my home. Been that way for twenty years." Michael is twenty-six.

5

The Fast Lane

WHERE ARE THE RED BALLOONS? *Where is my enGENE? For more than forty minutes, in between strokes, I've been looking for both—three giant blobs tied to a boat that's supposed to be my turning point. "When you reach that spot, it's almost halfway," I've been briefed. "You'll have completed the hardest section, and at that point the surf will assist you. You will swim as if you have an engine!" The advice is stern, the accent endearing. Ahmet Celik, our Turkish coordinator, pronounces it "enGENE," creating a mantra that loops endlessly through my brain: Where is my enGENE?*

Officially, I'm in a race, swimming against 431 competitors trying to beat me to Asia. It's a friendly competition. Just under half are foreigners like me: mostly Britons and Australians, some Russians, a handful of Americans, and a dozen-plus dashing Dutchmen ("responsible dads with busy jobs and big mortgages") who are swimming as a team to raise money for charity.

The rest are Turks, literally young Turks, with taut young bodies and irrepressible energy. Almost all are younger and faster than me, with records to match. Kate Bischof, a thirty-four-year-old Australian molecular biologist with the wiry frame of a teen, tells me she's just completed a twenty-kilometer (twelve-mile) race in the ocean off Perth. Bernie Stone, a fifty-two-year-old insurance project manager from Kent, England, likes to "swim the major gaps between continents." Last year he did the Gibraltar Straits (eighteen kilometers, or nearly eleven miles) and is practicing with an ice vest to swim from Diomede Island in Alaska to Russia. Lynne Tetley, a rosy-cheeked fifty-two-year-old from Yorkshire, came because her daughter wanted a companion. Lynne is diabetic and took up long-distance swimming when doctors told her she couldn't. She swam the English Channel twenty-five years ago. "Just to show that when they say I can't do it, I bloody well can," she says. "But I'm not in that shape anymore." I am utterly awed, and at the coaching clinic before our big swim, I trot over to Simon Murie, the tall, slender, Australian-born Briton whose company, SwimTrek, organized our swim, and report brightly that there's a Channel swimmer in our midst. "Lynn," he answers with patience, "there are a lot of Channel swimmers here." Including himself. Oops.

Me? I'm just trying to make it across. What makes that a special challenge is time: on this single day each year, the ships that usually ply these waters are stopped only for an hour and a half. If you don't hit the finish line by then, the safety boats will fish you out. Or before, if you're in trouble. At the prerace briefing, Ahmet assures us that fifty boats will be following. "I hope so!" shouts one nervous swimmer from the audience. "Follow me! Remember what I look like!" Never has ninety minutes seemed so short. Never has my swim involved so much preparation.

Before the event—early this morning—we were registered, examined (heart, blood pressure), numbered (I'm 327), tagged (with an electronic chip braceleted around the ankle) and capped (with special swim "bonnets" provided by the local Rotary Club: orange for foreigners, yellow for Turks), then transported across the strait by ferryboat at noon. The starting line is a pebbly beach where the water, a blissful 77 degrees, laps gently at our toes. Thank you, Poseidon. Last year's conditions were so foul, two-thirds of the swimmers didn't make it. And we've nervously watched blustery winds create three tense days of bumpy seas. Not today. The sea is so inviting, I think of Rupert Brooke, the English idealist who never made it to Gallipoli but wrote of "swimmers into cleanness leaping." I'm hoping we'll get the same.

The mood under the brilliant sun and paint-box sky is cheerful but edgy, a scrum of near-naked humans who have come together for three days of mutual passion but no idea what they're about to encounter. With our head-hugging caps (sorry, bonnets), skin-clinging suits, and bug-eyed goggles, we look like a colony of aliens about to greet the earthlings. I edge away from the crowd to find my own space. Swim your own swim, I've been told. Relax. Have fun. The orange flag lifts, and I take a deep breath. The gun goes off. The race is on.

Six supple needles weave orderly paths through an azure loom: fifty meters one way, fifty back again, across and back, across and back, a steady chain of flawless strokes from long, strong bodies. They are human submarines, missiles with manners, so in sync with the water in the outdoor pool, they barely ripple the surface. It is mesmerizing. The men and women of the Netherlands national swim team—two Olympic golds, one bronze already tucked away—are working out in Curaçao, a Caribbean reprieve from the raw snow and indoor haze of an Amsterdam winter. They're here to practice in the sun; I'm here, coincidentally, to improve my own it-hardly-seems-like-the-same-sport skills. The contrast, even on this blissful afternoon beneath a matching blue sky, with the rolling sea snuggling up under the deck, is sobering. As the Dutch journalist traveling with them informs me unapologetically, "This," nodding at his colleagues, "is swimming."

Yup.

I have come to this arid island near the coast of Venezuela for Swim Training Camp, a week of drills and distance training, another step in my plan to correct my stroke and crank up my pace. I am the rookie of the group, and not just because it's my first trip. Many of the other two dozen participants are triathletes, which means that they will, after an arduous hour and a half of sprints and sets at 7 AM, duck into a phone booth to reveal their Superman suits and then run and/or bike up to thirty-some miles in the withering heat.

All this while I'm back in my room reading the newspaper. When they return for the 4 PM ocean swim they can still fly past me.

Our chance encounter with the Dutch swimmers is an added bonus, a rare opportunity to watch excellence in action from poolside, not the TV screen.

The elite of any athletic discipline are exceptional, with their laser focus and purposed physiques. They are, in a word, different from you and me. Champion swimmers are especially distinctive. "Wide shoulders, thinner waist—some people have thicker thighs," the American Olympian Cullen Jones has told me, perfectly describing his own inverted-V shape as well. "But they're very defined. We're very, very defined. You should have a six-pack for sure." A cutout core where you can count every muscle: pecs, abs, obliques for openers; bulging lats that strain the straps of even the trimmest women; thick traps that broaden the back. At the 2010 Golden Goggles awards—professional swimming's version of the Oscars—three-time Olympic gold medalist Nancy Hogshead, still shapely in a floor-length, scoop-neck burgundy gown, looked out at the buff assembly of former and current athletes and said she loved the event because "I can come here and my arms are average!" As she flexed her right bicep, the audience roared its approval.

Height helps, too: Jones stands six foot five. Sun Yang, the Chinese teen who owns the world record for the four-hundred-meter free, is just under six foot six. American teenage sensation Missy Franklin is six foot one. Six-medal Olympian Ryan Lochte, six foot two. And then there's wingspan. Michael Phelps's arms reach out to six foot seven, three inches wider than he's tall. Others beat their height by six inches. Swimmers' long limbs tend to land in oversized hands

Michael Phelps in his Speedo LZR suit, 2008

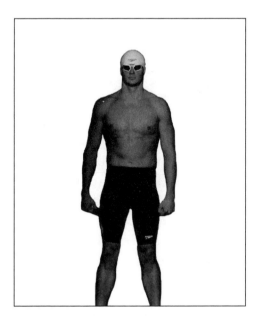

Ryan Lochte, ready for London, 2012

and feet, flipper-sized appendages (Franklin: size 13 shoes) that scoop up oceans of water. Their legs bow backwards; their gaits give away their strokes. Freestylers tend to be pigeon-toed; breaststrokers walk like ducks. They are flexible—very, very flexible. Phelps famously can bend his ankle so that it's almost flat in line with his leg, a perfect paddle. Olympian Dara Torres's toes look as if they function like fingers. Almost all are double-jointed where it counts, including the very cheerful and accommodating young Dutch woman completing her laps in the pool.

Ranomi Kromowidjodo, Dutch Olympian

"Oh, sure," Ranomi Kromowidjodo says, giggling, amused at my request to see her elbow in action. She nonchalantly twists it forward, an unnatural angle that would pop a bone from my skeleton but that helps her execute the freestyle that has made her a champion. At twenty-one, Kromowidjodo is the second fastest female swimmer in the world, finishing the fifty-meter freestyle in 24:27 during the World Championships in Shanghai in 2011. She lost the gold to Sweden's Therese Alshammar by 0.13 second. Kromowidjodo's teammate, Marleen Veldhuis, who touched the wall 0.22 second later for the bronze medal, is swimming one lane over here in Curaçao.

That's how you measure success in the swimming world: by slivers of time that are useless in, oh, everything else. Michael Phelps won his jaw-dropping eighth gold in Beijing in 2008 by 0.01 second.

It takes three times that long to blink. The fraction would be even more infinitesimal if the race clocks measured beyond two decimal points. In competition swimming, you don't round off the times the way you round off the pennies at the grocery store; you stretch every tick of the clock for every extra fingernail length you can wring out of it. In *Age Is Just a Number*, her book about her comeback at age forty-one, Dara Torres writes, "Swimmers know full well that every second has a beginning, a middle, and an end."

On this gentle, tropical afternoon, with the setting sun and the rising moon equidistant from the earth, and the infinity pool merging into the tiny creampuffs over the horizon, time is irrelevant. True, coach Jacco Verhaeren, an older but equally fit version of his talented charges, checks his stopwatch every lap or so, confirming the numbers he has already clocked in his head. But this part of the workout, their second two-hour swim of the day (bracketing an hour of dryland weights), is more about form and strength and endurance. They exchange kickboards with pull buoys to work on legs, then arms; they use snorkels to concentrate on balance without breathing; they grab bungee cords that are anchored on the deck to work their muscles even harder.

"Yes, it's tiring," Ranomi Kromowidjodo tells me as she towels off and unleashes her long black hair from its cap, gulping a swig of sports drink between perfect white teeth. "But I like to be in the water, to flow and just swim really slowly, easy. With my head submerged, it makes me feel like a fish." She recounts her addiction to the water, starting when she was just three. "I got a swimsuit, and I thought, 'I can swim!'" she recalls, laughing. "So I jumped into the pool. My mom gasped and said, 'Oh no!'" And then enrolled little Ranomi for her first swim lessons. By fifteen she was a European Junior champion. Now she spends eight or nine hours in the pool every day but Sunday, swimming some 45,000 meters (nearly 28 miles) a week. I ask if she

It's About Time

Ladies' race in London, 1906

Teri McKeever, head coach of the women's swim team at the University of California, Berkeley, is head coach of female swimmers for the 2012 Olympics. At fifty, she is the first woman ever to hold the job. *How does being a woman influence your coaching?*

I think good coaching is empowering your athlete—mentoring, not coercing. You see more partnershipping. You see more nurturing. But also, "Get your ass in gear!"

What's the secret to swimming?

It's not about overpowering your environment. The water isn't the same as the ground, where the harder you push on it, the more successful you'll be. I always tell the girls, if you get in a fight with the water, who wins? You have to find a way of working with it.

Why do you take your athletes to body-surf and paddle in the ocean?

So they can understand the power of the water. To get an awareness that there's energy and a rhythm there that, when you vary it, it hopefully. . . .

Makes you faster?

Well, I think so, but don't tell anyone!

You also take them to swim with dolphins, to observe penguins and whales.

I think you can learn by just watching. With dolphins, I said, "See if you can do what looks and feels like them. They have no bubbles coming off them. Try to mimic it."

Tell me something you love about swimming.

To be the first one in the pool when the sun is out, and you break that seal on the water, and then you can see your shadow on the bottom.

ever wakes up and does not want to work out. "No," she says quickly, echoing what her coach has already told me. "There is never a time I don't want to swim. I feel the water; I feel the power against my hands. I think of swimming and I. . . ." Her voice trails off as she tries to explain its significance in her life. "The swimming is most important. Everything else is secondary."

Kromowidjodo's next big performance will be at the London Olympics, where she hopes to win an individual gold medal—to join the one she won as part of the 4 x 100 freestyle relay team in Beijing in 2008. "You always want to have more," she explains. "Gold. It's human!"

Like most of the elite swimmers I meet, Ranomi Kromowidjodo avoids the bone-jangling impact of nonaquatic exercises. Most don't run, don't play basketball or tennis. One reason is muscle types: long, stretched fibers for the water that don't perform well on land. Another reason is floppy wrists and ankles. All that flexibility makes it hard to handle a racquet or hit the track without risk of injury. Rowdy Gaines, the affable three-time Olympic gold medalist who has broadened our understanding of swim races with his commentary for NBC, says he's awkward when he's not swimming. "I was a clodhopper on land," he tells me. "In high school I tried out for five sports—football, basketball, baseball, tennis, golf." Didn't make any of the cuts. "Look at *The Superstars*," he adds, citing the TV program forcing athletes to compete outside their own specialty. "Swimmers always finished dead last. I did." Today Gaines still swims almost every day. "I was born and raised in Florida, so I grew up with water all around me," he says. "I learned to swim before I could walk. I love the feeling of being in the water."

Although swimming was not part of the original Olympics, it has been a mainstay of the modern Games since they reappeared in Athens in 1896. During the mid-nineteenth century, top British champions regularly solicited competitors with classified ads in the

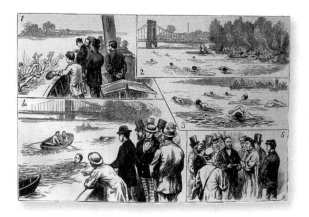

Racing in the Thames, London, 1874

newspaper. They were adult play dates for money prizes, accompanied by such heavy betting—it was "rife," one source reported, "of more importance than the swimming"—that abolishing it was one of the first orders of business when an amateur swimming society was formed.

How fast is fast?

In the past three decades, in the race usually considered that of the fastest swimmer in the world (fifty-meter free), male elite swimmers have shaved almost 2 seconds off the record; females, more than 2 seconds. In swimming, that's huge. Just for comparison, Mark Spitz swam the hundred-meter fly in 47.9 for one of his 1972 gold medals. The record today is 44.1. Olympian (and future Tarzan) Johnny Weissmuller made headlines around the globe when he broke the 1-minute mark for the hundred-meter freestyle (held by another American, Duke Kahanamoku) in 1922. Weissmuller's time was 58.6. Today's world record is 46.91. I could go on.

And the swimmers will, in their endless race to lower the times. "It's so cool to be able to push my body as far as it can go," explains Nathan Adrian, a week before his twenty-third birthday. Already an Olympic gold medalist, he tells me that lifting more weights, doing more reps, "is a rush of endorphins. That's why I do it." When I ask if his love of swimming is all about going faster, his handsome face widens into a huge grin. "Yeah! Obviously! What else would it be about?" And why does he like going fast? Nathan, a pre-med graduate of the University of California, Berkeley, pauses playfully and says, "I don't know. Is that a Darwinian question?" Then he goes on: "It's just testing myself against the rest of the world. We all swim freestyle differently—Michael [Phelps], Ryan [Lochte], myself. It's testing my race strategy, my body, my prep, my physiology against theirs. And that's exciting. Look at little kids—they race all the time. We're just like big little kids with technology behind our backs!"

Indeed, strokes that evolved haphazardly in recent centuries have been honed by calculated research. And a modern world obsessed with fins on cars and rockets to the moon has inevitably applied the same aerodynamic inquiry to its human torpedoes. Indiana's Counsilman used early underwater films to analyze swimmers' movements, pointing out that stroke mechanics, not just brute force, could improve a swimmer's speed. Other inquiries helped lead to an explosion of tests and devices that have measured virtually every pore and tic of the body to shave milliseconds off one's time. Swimmers have been dropped into giant flumes, or streams of current, to test their stroke efficiency, and diodes mounted on their limbs have tracked the trajectory of their arms. Their dives and grips off the starting block, as well as the exact distance fingers should be spread to pull the most water have all been measured and compared. The science behind the latter is called the "boundary layer," which "closes up" the gaps the way a mesh fly swatter acts like a solid paddle.

Optimally, your fingers should be exactly six millimeters apart. Unfortunately, that's so small that it's very hard to maintain. So most swimmers I know keep their hands almost flat, fingers almost together, thumb apart. Never cup your hand.

The emphasis on science has made today's swimmers fluent in the language of fluid dynamics. Many speak with authority about the forces of propulsion and lift and thrust, and about the enemy, drag, the friction that puts on the brakes. Racers will do anything to avoid drag: shave, slither, and don sleek suits. Drag can be the difference between gold and silver. Drag can really be a drag. Learning about it has changed the way we stroke.

In the late 1960s, Doc Counsilman's research on drag convinced freestylers to use the so-called S-stroke. That's where you curve your leading arm in toward the body before moving it back out past the hip for recovery. It was based on an effect in physics called Bernoulli's Principle, and it was supposed to work because lift-based thrust—pushing water perpendicular to the body—was more effective than drag-based thrust—pushing water back parallel to the body. The prime example is the boat: when you paddle, it's drag; when the propeller rotates, it's lift. Which one gets you there faster? A number of coaches voted for lift, and the S-shaped arm stroke, rather than the straight-back deep catch, took over. That was then. A generation or so later, the thinking is different.

"The nice thing about computational modeling is that we can actually test some of these things," explains Rajat Mittal of the Department of Mechanical Engineering at Johns Hopkins University. "So we got underwater video of some Olympic athletes using both strokes, and we simulated both." That simple sentence belies hours of painstak-

Diver's tomb, Paestum

Native American swimmers as seen by George Catlin

Swim race in the Lhasa River from a mural in the Potala Palace, Tibet, late seventeenth century

Japanese war hero Sergeant Kawasaki swims across a rain-swollen river during the Sino-Japanese War, 1894.

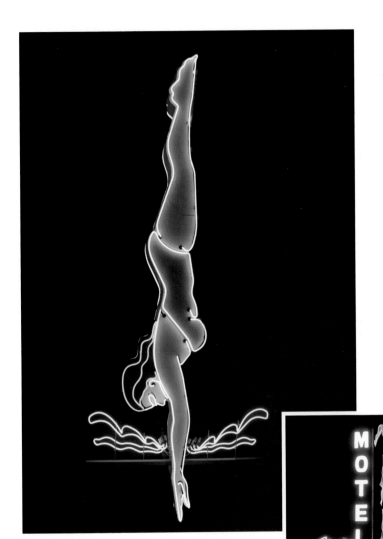

She was the queen of the desert from the moment the
sign first went up in 1960: the neon diving lady,
elegantly plunging into a splash of turquoise at the
Starlite Motel in Mesa, Arizona. Night after night, twenty times a minute,
she beckoned travelers to its refreshing swimming pool. When a violent
hailstorm destroyed the landmark in 2010, a passionate group of preserva-
tionists began raising private money and donations of material to restore the
swimmer to her longtime perch. The cosmetic surgery was a success. Awaiting
resurrection in the warehouse, the final figure in the sequence—more than
sixteen feet tall—looks even more gorgeous in her close-up at age fifty-one.

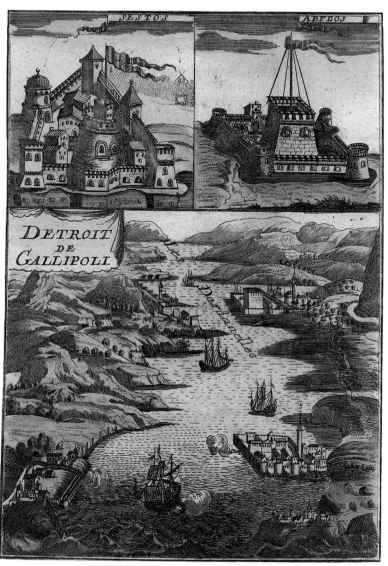

Antique map of the Hellespont/Dardanelles ("Detroit," or Straits, of Gallipoli) showing the castles of Sestos and Abydos, 1719

The Hellespont, looking north from the Asian side

How Leander might have seen the Hellespont during his nightly swims

Waiting for the gun on race day

We're off!

That's me, early in the race. The finish line is far off to the right.

The Course, as captured by Google.

Swimming to the finish line

#1 . . . and only

Have I shown you my medal?

ing research, based on their ability to analyze how water flows past the body. Dr. Mittal and his team animated their study using the same computer program that gave us the movie *Shrek*. What they learned was no fantasy. "We found that the deep catch [drag-based] is definitely superior," he tells me. "And I tried it out myself. It does seem to work better." Dr. Mittal, a recreational lap swimmer who entertains himself in the pool by thinking about the drag he might be creating, adds one more twist to the story. "Even the deep catch actually produces quite a bit of thrust from lift," he says, "so in some sense half the theory was true! There is some amount of lateral motion in the arms as you complete the stroke. We'll send it in to a swimming journal."

Dr. Mittal first came to the swim world's attention with a study funded by USA Swimming that analyzed American Olympians' use of the dolphin kick, a major mechanical influence on modern competitive swimming. Now he's studying fish, trying to learn what kind of noise a fish makes when it swims and how that might relate to human swimming efficiency. He wants to know how fish use their pectoral fins to swim so efficiently; what makes their fins similar to butterfly wings; why dolphins work at 60 percent efficiency in the water and humans only 11 to 12 percent. "A lot of the dolphin's efficiency is due to its beautifully streamlined shape," he explains. "And if we could just wear a suit that would make us have the shape of a dolphin, we'd recover quite a bit of that efficiency."

Dr. Mittal also wonders why dolphins' speed seems to defy physics. "The amount of power they're swimming at seems to far exceed the muscle power of the animal," he says. The meditation turns to fact. "Many fish and cetaceans, and especially the dolphin, exude some kind of mucous from their pores, a little slime layer." Polymer drag reduction, he calls it. He says it really works, and that both the Navy and DARPA are spending millions to see if it can apply to marine vehicles. Wait till the coaches hear about that one.

Gains in the lane also come from the pool itself. Deep water is faster; deeper gutters mean less splash-back; wider lane lines mean calmer waters. Calm is good. The fastest swimmers get to swim in the middle because there's less turbulence from competitors. And those colorful markers dividing one lane from another are not just colorful markers: they're scientifically engineered wave-destroyers to keep the pool from becoming a foamy water park. The patent on the ones you see at your local Y or school is likely held by Adolph Kiefer, the indefatigable Olympian (he won gold at the Berlin Olympics in 1936) and champion of all things swimming (the company he founded in Illinois supplies much of the nation's aquatic gear) who still swims daily in his nineties.

All those refinements make the swimmers faster and the meets more exciting, which leads to new records and, the promoters hope, bigger audiences. But they're tough to attract. Swim meets are inherently hard to follow—all you see is a head, arms, the froth of a kick. Underwater cameras help, with clock-stopping images of fingertip touches, but you never get the mid-race close-up of the athlete's face, can't get behind the goggles to focus on how he or she might be feeling.

That's why, in the tradition of the late, great Roone Arledge, the best television sports programming focuses on the athletes' stories, to engage the viewer with what's going on inside that swim-capped head. And with so many sports competing for the attention of a finite audience, it also helps if the team wins. "My philosophy has been to make swimming the centerpiece of prime time," says Dick Ebersol, the innovative executive producer of NBC's Olympics coverage for twenty years and now a consultant for the 2012 games. "With swimming, you get American winners." He puts his faith in USA Swimming, which governs and promotes the sport, to identify and nourish champions. It "has arguably the best grassroots organ-

Racing in the Thames, London, 1908

ization of any Olympic sport in the US," Ebersol says. As a result, "you can rely on the swimmers."

If they get to that level, they are a breed apart. "The Olympians in almost every single sport are mutants," a coach tells me with complete awe. "They're at the far end of the bell curve. And they have the perfect body type, the perfect physio type, and the perfect mind. Did you see *The King's Speech*? Remember where he tells him, 'It's not about the mechanics'? You know, you get to a certain point, and it's not about the mechanics. That's what separates the Olympians. Do they have the heart and mind? And can they be there on that stage and perform at that minute?"

They call it "neck up"—because so many contests are won or lost in the head. Prerace tactics can rattle the brain. "I told everyone in the wait room I was going to 'false start,'" confesses Donna de-Varona, whose two gold medals at the 1964 Olympics capped her spectacular teenage swimming career. "And I did." She reminds me that the rules used to allow two false starts—where you go off before the gun—and that she took full advantage. "I wanted to get wet. It made me feel close to the water, and I could breathe better," she says. She also admits that it was "very self-centered." Anything out of the ordinary can unsettle finely tuned racers, shaking them out of their concentration. Today a false start gets you disqualified. De-Varona would have prevailed without it. "It's all about speed," she says, wincing at the memories. "You're a Formula One race car. Competitive swimming is the ability to push the pain threshold further in every way."

For some, it's life changing. Mel Stewart, who won two golds and one bronze in the 1992 Olympics, today is a passionate swimming promoter and blogger. But after his victories he stopped swimming for ten years. "There was so much pressure, so many tears," he says. "When I finally made it, it wasn't joy—it was relief. I maybe swam three hours a year for those ten years afterwards."

New York Times sports writer Karen Crouse, a former competitor herself, understands the emotional cost of a career in the water. "I came into college thinking swimmers were the most well-adjusted, balanced, sane individuals. But I saw so much dysfunction—I didn't have the life experience to understand that winning isn't normal. And now that I'm grown up and covering athletes day after day after day, it is really so rare I see a top-level athlete who I would say is a well-balanced individual. There's usually some hole in their lives they're trying to fill through athletic achievement. I used to feel such regret that I'd never become the swimmer I wanted to be; now I'm thinking I just didn't have enough dysfunction."

The dissonance between the years of Olympic glory (when "you made the water boil and the whole world hold its breath") and the reality of resurfacing in the nonswimming world is starkly dramatized in *Amphibians*, a well-reviewed play recently staged in an abandoned London pool. Creator-director Cressida Brown based it on interviews with past and present athletes, and while the pool is empty, the limber actors, clad in bathing suits and caps, writhe in the virtual water like a team of terrified minnows. "Lane Six is my name," announces one, stripped of humanity after a lifetime of practice as a teenager. "You're first, second, third, or you're nothing," says another. "There is only time and water, the race and the finish, the black line."

For Cullen Jones, the drama is his life. Like most sprinters, he holds his breath for the entire twenty-one seconds of the fifty-meter freestyle. Sure, you are thinking; I can hold my breath for twenty-one seconds. Easy. Oh yeah? While trying to cover the same territory on your belly that a quarterback races from the fifty-yard line? "You go from very, very comfortable to very, very uncomfortable very, very fast." Jones tells me. "Any time that you are missing a bus and you run for the bus, you know that winded, tired, that almost-choking feeling in your chest? That's what I have to learn to live with. My race is twenty-one seconds. By the first five seconds, I'm hurting. And I'm going, and halfway, you're like, GASP—you're like, 'I gotta get in, gotta get in.'" I ask if the pain is centered in his lungs. "Everything. It's everything. You're gonna be kicking so hard your legs are burning. Your arms are moving; your arms are gonna get tired, especially when you're pulling water. You're literally pulling yourself up through the water and throwing it back behind you." He shakes his head at the thought.

"Do you swim for pleasure now?"

"Not right now. I don't think any of us really do," he says. A smile returns. "I'm in the pool for four to six hours every day, and then I'm lifting weights on top of that. And sometimes on a Saturday, I'll sleep for a couple of hours, and friends come by and say, 'Hey, see you in the pool,' and I'm like, 'No, I'll stay dry. I want to be dry for the next twenty-four hours.'"

Infinity in the Caribbean

On the morning I enter the water in Curaçao—my first workout in a rectangle fifty meters long—I understand why it's called an infinity pool. The barely visible far wall seems planted in another hemisphere. Olympians demolish this distance in roughly twenty-five strokes (that's left one, right two, left three, and so on). I will be lucky to triple that. I am in the Doug Stern pool at Lion's Dive and Beach Resort, an unpretentious, aquacentric hotel that has become a familiar home to my group. The adventure was begun several decades ago by Stern, a gifted New York coach who was, by all accounts, a born teacher, a deeply inspiring leader, a guy who could make anyone a better swimmer and a better person. The boom in triathlons brought him waves of talented runners and cyclers eager to learn, or perfect, that third leg. His charisma brought them back year after year. Although Stern died in 2007, the winter tradition continues in the pool now named for him, with many of his followers, two other swim instructors, and a few first-timers.

We begin with pyramids—increasing sets of fifty, one hundred, up to two hundred meters, then down again. We do one-armed drills to improve our pull then kickboard lengths to get the legs going. We work on endurance by breathing every stroke, then every third stroke, then—well, I still can't do that part of it for long. I thought I had breathing down—it is, after all, something I've been doing for a lot of years—unconsciously on land, with barely a thought in the water. Turns out, you need to think about it. "Swimming is the only sport where you have to actively focus on when you do breathe, or else bad things happen," says Scott Bay, coach chair for US Masters Swimming. In a telephone conversation several months later, he tells me that the problem starts when "we're taught, at a really early age, to take a deep breath and hold it, then go underwater. We tend to stick with that all of our lives." The consequences can be very disruptive. "If you hold your breath for just half

How to Breathe, 1624

a second," Bay goes on, "you're flexing all your muscles in your core, especially the diaphragm, just to hold that breath. And every time you flex a muscle, it's going to burn some oxygen. So those core muscles are burning oxygen for fuel, taking oxygen out of the blood stream rather than putting it in." And depriving the muscles that need it to swim. "Don't hold your breath," he advises. "Slowly exhale when your face is in the water. You want to try to breathe as normally and rhythmically as possible."

Not too normally. Once, during a USMS class when we are doing "lungbusters"—lengths of the pool underwater, without breathing, to increase our endurance—I find myself so relaxed, feeling so "normal" as I glide along, with the pretty, pale blue tiles beneath me, I momentarily forget I am human and try to breathe in. When my nonexistent gills don't function, I shoot up to the surface to gulp some air. In extreme cases, that's called shallow-water blackout and can be deadly. With me, it was just dumb.

Back in Curaçao, I can't say I'm having fun yet. Can't figure out why I'm doing racing sprints when I'm just trying to improve my long-distance performance. Turns out, learning to go fast complements tweaking your technique. You need to do both. And within a day or so I am feeling more comfortable—still lagging behind most, but sometimes swimming alongside or ahead of a few others. Our patient but very persistent coaches, Boris Talan and Vlad Bartchouk, best buddies from their time as Russian swim stars, pinpoint my challenges: I need to curve my wrists downward, soften my left leg, and break the water slightly in the kick. But I am learning. And yes, Boris agrees, I have a very strong breaststroke.

The folks in my lane, and the lanes next to us, are nothing but supportive. They are also remarkably diverse: from Eastern Canada to the Northwest Coast; from Michigan and Maryland and Brooklyn, New York. They are men and women, with and without mates, from their thirties to their late seventies. Only a few fit the body type of the pros. There is a veterinarian, an advertising executive, a government manager, a sculptor, two retired schoolteachers. And while they are all very proficient in the water and attached to it, they don't always love it unconditionally.

"I think swimming hurts too much. You have to work so hard at it," confesses Irene Pawley-Kennedy, forty-four, a slender, energetic former gymnast who only started swimming in 2001. But she's happy to put in the work, teaching high school and age-group swimming and using her strong stroke in long-distance competitions in the lakes of Michigan. She's here with her husband, Andy, a beefy six foot two with a monster kick behind his powerful freestyle. At dinner one evening after our afternoon ocean swim—a taxing hour in rolling swells that had me gasping despite the fins strengthening my kick—Irene and Andy joke about how much fun it was to time their strokes to the waves. I think how nice it would be to have that much control.

For many of these swimmers, it is less a sport than a discipline, less a workout than a way of life. Malonnie Kinnison, a radiologist, is a champion cyclist and triathlete who has been swimming since she was an infant. "Swimming was like life," she tells me. "It was different every day. You'd have days where you'd own the water; it was just there for you. Other days it was just like swimming in mud." Was that about you or the water?, I ask. "Me!" she responds. "Swimming is the way you see yourself, your life. It's just the way you look at it. It could all be working, and you hope that day will be race day.

"Air," she goes on, "doesn't do it—but in water, you're totally surrounded by the medium. Especially when everything is working. You're just gliding along, and you say, 'Wow, this is it!'" She thinks what sets swimming apart is the breathing. "You really get into it because you have to. It's a matter of life or death. You can run without thinking so much about it. But you cannot swim without controlling your breath. It's the breath of life."

Or the breath of peace. Sara Widenhouse is here from North Carolina. She learned to swim as a child in the chilly sea off Rhode Island and then gave it up when she moved south to the mountains. But after her son turned two, she started doing laps again and discovered, "Wow! It's quiet in the pool! It was like a big time-out." Swimming also saved her during a recent bout with a very rare form of appendix cancer. "When I was going through chemo, swimming counterbalanced the hours of being tied to a drip," she tells me. "It was like a prize, a dream that kept me going. It made me feel like I was winning." When I speak with her after our trip, she is even more grateful. "It was an amazing gift. I shed my patient issues and did things I did not know I was capable of. Swimming makes me feel like I'm really living the life I want. It's the most rewarding activity I do, and it's helped me physically, emotionally, and spiritually."

Nothing stops them. Judy Reibert, a former New York cable TV executive, once swam down the Hudson River and nearly found herself on the way to Wall Street because the currents almost kept her from hitting the landing spot. Kate Pennell, an advertising manager who also corrals the unruly gang with verve and efficiency, encountered a clear, round jellyfish during a swim to Malta that gave her a scar lasting seven months. Ray Plotecia, a former surfer (and Malonnie's husband), found his first triathlon swim, in the Severn River at Annapolis, terrifying: "The guns go off; there are hundreds of people thrashing about; it's as if you're surrounded by piranha. I couldn't put my face in the water. Could I go back to shore? The distance—half a mile out, half a mile back—looked huge. But I did the breaststroke, eased in the crawl, and made it. Then I realized I could do anything." He has since completed the Ironman/Hawaii five times.

Another of my swim campmates is Dr. Oliver Sacks, the brilliant author and neurologist. To this group, he's Oliver the swimmer—the onetime West Coast weightlifting champ whose diminished physique at seventy-seven has not restrained his enthusiasm for the activity he loves most in the world. He has been a water baby (his term) since childhood and has written and spoken eloquently on "the essential rightness about swimming. . . . I never knew anything so powerfully, so healthily euphoriant," he's said. In Curaçao, Oliver is more fragile than he'd like but shows up for every drill and ocean outing. And when he slips into the water, he is very strong indeed. One afternoon while we are snorkeling together, a rare free-swim in the arms of a secluded cove, he tells me, "I wish I could spend my life in the water. I feel much more confident here." Later, after reading a passage aloud from one of his books to the group gathered around him on the beach—an annual rite that captivates everyone—he talks about his newest swimming milestones: "A longer stroke," he announces. "And bilateral breathing. For a year it seemed so artificial—now it feels natural. One year." The lesson? "The plasticity of the human brain. You can teach an old dog new tricks. You continue to learn until you die."

I think about that the next day, as I am about to leave Curaçao to return home: my arms are aching, my shoulders stiff. It is the first time I have ever hurt from swimming, which means I am doing something either very right or very wrong. I like to think it's the former, that by pushing my body to explore a more intense form of this activity, I am discovering more about myself.

One of the swimming professors at Indiana told me he likes the tough Masters workout because "the social component makes you work harder. In rest periods, you're lane pals, and it makes it a much better experience. I am," he says, "happy in my lane." I mention that I'm not, that the faster swimmers are frustrating to me, that being passed is very humbling. "So is parenting," he says.

There it is again: swimming as life. You may never get either one totally right. But you can, as Oliver Sacks says, always learn.

Liquid Silk

Syndicated health columnist Judy Foreman, who did her first flip turn at fifty-nine, placed sixth in the fifty-meter backstroke at the 2011 US Masters Nationals meet in Mesa, Arizona, at the age of sixty-seven. The competition would have been unthinkable a little over a decade ago. "I had just left the *Boston Globe*," she recalls. "And I missed the camaraderie. So I joined USMS and started swimming three days a week, at noon. The first year or so it took courage: it was so intense. I swam in the slow lane—still do—with snorkel and flippers. I thought, 'When is this workout going to be over?' Now I find it delightful to have something physical that I'm getting better at." Water, she says, is "liquid silk." Swimming is "the only place I feel valued for being old." At Nationals, she was invigorated as much by the crowd as by the race. When it was over, "everybody, the whole 1,800 of us, stood and cheered for some ninety-year-old guy who finished his race!"

6

Go with the Flow

STILL NO RED BALLOONS, *at least not from my frog's-eye view of the sea. I check my watch and realize I've been at it for more than forty-five minutes. Will I finish in time if I can't find the boat? That's one of the challenges of open-water swimming: without markers, you can't read distance. The field of blue seems to stretch on forever. And that's just across. Down is another problem. It's too deep to see the bottom, maybe three hundred feet beneath me, and there are no lane lines to keep me straight. No walls to push off. Not to mention the fact that I am sharing someone else's territory, someone who might not be terribly friendly. Someone, or something, that now shows up unexpectedly.*

"Yuck!" The fingers of my left hand strike Jell-O—a slimy mass that feels like dessert. I retract my arm like a bullet and peer into the brine: it's a jellyfish, a transparent, undulating disk some four inches in diameter that, I am relieved to discover, seems equally repelled by me. It scoots away benignly. We've all been obsessing about jellyfish, daily discussing the odds of long, poisonous stingers plaguing our route. The boats, we're assured, carry plenty of vinegar to treat the afflicted. Small consolation. As it turns out, we're lucky—no purple nasties this day, just these colorless little critters,

who intermittently become my companions for the crossing. Half a dozen times my eyes fasten on a small cluster—a class, not a school, of jellies, shimmering in shafts of sunlight. One grander specimen, at least ten inches across, whirls around like a flying saucer. It's dreamy and makes me smile. Then I refocus.

This is not Leander's route. For one thing, he swam at night, while we splash across in splendid sun. For another, he, mythologically, shot straight from his home in the ancient Asian city of Abydos to the tower where Hero lived in European Sestos, a distance that used to measure less than a mile, according to the first-century geographer Strabo. Since both cities are long gone, and the coastline has substantially eroded, our journey follows a slightly different path, governed less by myth than by nature.

"There are two sets of currents," Ahmet told us at the briefing, projecting a giant diagram with unambiguous arrows. "The warm water from the Mediterranean flows north and is pushed under by the cold water from the Black Sea flowing south." The result: a narrow pair of upward flowing forces along each coast flanking a broader and much faster downward force in the middle. It is too strong to permit a simple, point-to-point crossing, which would only be about a mile. Instead, we are routed along a sweeping arc from the town of Eceabat, on the European side, slightly northeast to compensate for the currents, then southeast along the shore to the finish line at Canakkale, the quiet Asian seaport where we are staying. Canakkale's main tourist attraction is the gigantic wooden horse used in the Brad Pitt movie Troy, a campy souvenir of an artifact that likely never existed from a film that was not shot here. This is no Hollywood-on-the-Hellespont, simply where we will end up if we follow the squiggly path. Four times longer than the straight shot across, it is the only smart choice. "If you go in a straight line, very few will complete the course," Ahmet cautions over and over again. "You can be dragged out of the strait. You can easily underestimate the current. And if you're in it, and find yourself south of the finish point, it is almost impossible to swim back. Don't try. Accept the help of the boats." Just in case we don't catch his drift, he concludes ominously, "You must swim this course. If not, you will wind up . . . [pause for dramatic effect] . . . somewhere else." Some of the audience giggle. I busily memorize the diagram.

I have been obsessed by maps since I signed up for this event, repeatedly pulling up the location on Google Earth and tracing my finger across these waters. It seemed *to make sense sitting at home in New York; the idea of crossing open water felt both exotic and sensible. A destination swim. Now that I'm in it, it's a lot bigger than my fingertip. But I like the sense of place, the knowledge that I'm not bouncing back and forth between walls, just going forth to another continent. As Simon Murie of SwimTrek has told me, "It's about the idea of the journey. When you've done it, you can see where you came from. That's the great thing about open-water swimming: you finish somewhere different. In a pool, you finish where you started."*

Not that there's anything wrong with swimming pools. In the ongoing debate over where best to swim—the untamed blue waters that define our planet or the boxed-in beauty of pools—I'm an equal-opportunity addict. And while I trained for the Hellespont mostly by swimming long distances in the bay and the ocean off the eastern end of New York's Long Island, my final postevent workouts were in the warm crystal waters of the peaceful pool at the Four Seasons Hotel in Istanbul, a blue-tiled oasis snuggled so close to the Bosporus, I imagined myself swimming across that fabled waterway, too.

Pools glisten in the sun; they illuminate a dreary yard; they play with lines and light, as the wavy reflections of sun in water animate the straight walls. Shadows and shimmering patterns make endless new designs, always in motion, as the artist David Hockney brilliantly captured in swimming-pool paintings and collages that have redefined the color blue. Pools are pure, a simple shape that traps nature's force for our benefit. We think differently about water when it's made accessible. It's a surprise, a safe haven in the most improbable places. One proposal for the redevelopment of New York's abandoned High Line railway imagined the entire track as a swimming pool, a mile-long ribbon of blue winding above the city. One very long lap. The author of a history of swimming pools doctored a photo to add a diving board to the reflecting pool at the Lincoln Memorial in Washington, DC. Suddenly it graduates from decoration to invitation: you want to plunge in. (Don't: It's too shallow. Also illegal.)

Icy hair, warm water in Utah

At a health club in Manhattan's East Side, I swam in a pool beneath a skylight so vast, I could count the buildings and, in my mind's eye, swim down, then up Second Avenue. Cars can't even do that. In Deer Valley, Utah, I gathered up my granddaughters and took a dip amid the steam of the 100-degree pool at the Stein Erikson Lodge, a blissful way to repair the muscle damage of a day on the trails. Watching skiers slide by was otherworldly; as eleven-year-old Sammy pointed out, "Lynn, your hair is frozen!"

Seeing pools from an airplane makes me want to parachute in. They are modern oases, turquoise rectangles in the urban desert. Lawmakers find them even more valuable. In 2010, when Greece first awoke to its dire financial situation, satellite photos of swimming pools in the suburbs helped identify scofflaws who were not paying taxes on them.

Pools were an ancient pleasure as well. Public baths, sometimes used for swimming, dotted the Roman Empire, vital centers of social discourse before they devolved into playgrounds of debauchery. In Rome, Pliny the Younger had a heated pool from which he could see the sea. Seneca the Younger lived up to his Stoic principles by bathing only in cold water and criticizing his colleagues for disparaging anything but a pool lined with fancy marble. But the biggest pool empire of that world was built by the erratic first-century BCE dictator, Herod the Great, whose indoor and outdoor tanks can be seen in Israel from the top of Masada to the ramparts of old Jerusalem. The archeological evidence of this master builder's monuments are dazzling. Herod built a 250-meter pool at his palace in Jericho, now in Jordan, which might have been used for sailing. Also for a drowning. The maniacal king was so identified with the structures, in the 1970s Broadway hit *Jesus Christ, Superstar*, the character of Herod challenges Jesus to "walk across my swimming pool," an irreverent allusion that is at least rooted in historic real estate.

Overlooking Herod's "public immersion pool," Masada

Like swimming itself, the pool as a popular addition to courtyard or backyard disappeared from Western history after the fall of Rome. In the eighteenth century, the first floating tanks drifted on barges down the River Seine. The Germans and Austrians quickly built their own. In Germany, King Ludwig II, who would ultimately be known by the adjective "mad," included a pool in his fairy-tale Neuschwanstein Castle. Meanwhile, they started digging in England, where by the 1850s enough pools existed to feed the growing passion for the sport. In the United States, swimming baths came to the big cities, and the first public swimming pool may have been the one opened in Brookline, Massachusetts, in 1897—a grand indoor tank that paid homage to Leander, among others, on its tiled walls.

Women's Day at a New York Swimming Bath, 1882

In California, William Randolph Hearst set a new standard with his Roman-style pools (designed by architect Julia Morgan) at San Simeon, a modern palace. By the 1930s, swimming pools had moved from the private estates of Vanderbilts and Morgans on the East Coast to the mansions of movie stars on the West. They were a symbol of luxury, the exclusive province of royalty and the rich. "Hollywood? Oh, what a life!," proclaimed actor Dick Powell in the 1937 movie *Hollywood Hotel.* "Falling in and out of swimming pools."

Liberace and Frank Sinatra swam in pools shaped like pianos; Jayne Mansfield, a heart. Joan Fontaine had a pool with an island in the middle; Mary Pickford and Douglas Fairbanks could fit a canoe in theirs.

Liberace and his piano pool

Pools became freeform with the availability of the more moldable gunnite, leading to specimens shaped like, of all things, kidneys. A Florida dentist had a pool that looked like a molar; a seafood wholesaler, a blue crab. Angles returned with lap pools, an invention of the 1970s. And while California remained the swimming-pool capital of the country, the suburbanization of America in the late 1950s suddenly made pools affordable for more mainstream citizens. In 1948, there were 2,500 residential swimming pools in the United States; in 1957, 57,000. It was just the beginning.

Today the more than 10 million Americans with private pools are using them for far more than just swimming. "I think the biggest trend is that people these days want more than a pool," says Dan Johnson, a Florida builder who operates out of Sarasota. "When I got into the business, if you gave them a fifteen-by-thirty kidney-shaped pool, they were thrilled. Today, almost no pool goes in without a water feature. They want to see the water move; they want to hear it move; they want it to dance, to turn colors at night." One of his most popular features, he says, is the rain curtain: "A laminar jet creates a stream so perfect, it looks like a neon tube. And I can actually tune the sound." Johnson adds that people originally just wanted to get wet, to splash around, "happy as a lark. Now, getting wet isn't enough."

I ask if people actually swim in their pools these days. "The vast majority don't!" Johnson replies, astonished. "I'd guess less than 20 percent. I'd bet my salary on it." So what do they do there? "We build a lot of benches in pools, like living rooms," he explains. "Also tables, against the side wall, and on the other side, bar stools. They sit down

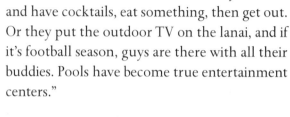

and have cocktails, eat something, then get out. Or they put the outdoor TV on the lanai, and if it's football season, guys are there with all their buddies. Pools have become true entertainment centers."

Pool, bar, state-of-the-art kitchen, fireplace, rope swings, and waterfalls in Asheville, N.C. "It has changed the way our family spends time together," say the owners, the parents of four children.

Dick Covert, whose Richmond, Virginia–based Masters Pools Guild connects high-end pool builders around the world, says the trend began after 9/11, "when a lot of people started saying, 'Travel is not safe; it's hectic; it's inconvenient. We're going to create our own environment in our house.'" So they turned their backyards into mini-resorts, with outdoor kitchens and waterfalls and other amenities. "Outdoor living has become a way of life," he says, "and the pool area has become another room in their home." He describes a home in Oklahoma City where the pool area contains "a lazy river—like at a resort, where you can float in an inner tube, several hundred yards long.

There's a lot of land in Oklahoma!" And he says most outdoor kitchens contain "a Viking-type setup to cook, grill, or make the meal completely outdoors. There's also generally a lounge area, with the TV. It's really where they live."

His customers, says Covert, also swim. "They want twenty-five meters for laps. And one of our vendors does a really good business in in-pool bicycles and treadmills." He's also seen his share of odd designs, especially in Nashville. "I saw a pool shaped like a record with an island in the middle. And a piano. And one like a *Star Trek* deal." Another trend, he says, is the natural pool—building something that looks as if it belongs there. "We see a lot where you can walk down what we call 'zero entry,' or beach entry," he explains. "It's just like going in from the beach. And we have one in Illinois that looked like a winter scene with snow, a gorgeous pond in the winter—but not frozen, because they kept it heated." Covert believes that pools are an escape. "People see them as a total change from the hectic world we live in. When you go into your backyard and all of a sudden you're in a quiet place with running water, you hear the fountain—well, you just begin to relax. After you're tied in knots all day long, working, on the telephone, on the computer, a pool has a calming effect on people." A former lifeguard who still enjoys the water himself, Dick Covert prefers the pool to the ocean. "I don't like the salt; I don't like the creatures. In the ocean you have to struggle. In a pool I can just float!"

On the other hand, swimming pools are a round trip to nowhere, over and over again. The narrator of a novel about a racer says, "Swimming back through your own wake you always feared that you'd crash into yourself coming the other way. They should have built pools that expanded or contracted to the required length, or huge circular ones in which you'd spiral round until you reached the center."

Autographed postcard of Ederle, slathered against the elements as she enters the Channel. Note her signature: "Swimmingly yours, Trudy Ederle."

"I don't like pools," SwimTrek's Simon Murie admits. "In an indoor pool, every day is the same. It's like McDonald's—the same meal wherever you are. But go to a local café, and every meal will be different. That's the beauty of open-water swimming: each day is different."

Annette Kellerman was more blunt. "Swimming under a roof to me is like big game hunting in a zoo. All legitimate fascination goes."

Open-water swimming is not for the faint of heart or the easily chilled. One of the founders of the wild swimming movement in Britain, where hardy souls seek the least hospitable swimming holes, advises, "You must get in with purpose. Don't just stand there dipping your toe and wondering if it's warm enough, because if you are in Britain chances are it won't be."

Captain Webb's achievement
struck such a chord,
he lived on as a popular
matchbox brand.

Especially if you're dipping that toe into the English Channel. The water measured a nippy 61 degrees when Gertrude Ederle struck out in 1926. And that was just the temperature at the surface, in August, when the icy waters heated up. It is so volatile, you can see the swirling currents; so unpredictable, you can start in a lake and soon be battered by crushing swells; so demonic, the turn of the tide can keep you from your goal, as Ederle discovered just off-shore of Kent. "I felt as if the sea were pulling me right away from England," she said later.

So what's the draw? Why do people still grease themselves up, gather a GPS-directed crew, dodge oil tankers, and agree to be fed from cups dangled at the end of a stick (no touching the boat or a human, or you're disqualified)? Why has the goal line moved from just crossing the perilous sleeve, as the French call it, to crossing it three times in a row, for which the record is now twenty-eight hours, twenty-one minutes, just eight hours longer than it took Matthew Webb to make it one way? The answer is not, as mountaineer George Mallory said of climbing Mount Everest, "Because it's there." "You don't swim the Channel because *it's* there: you swim it because *you* are," writes Kathy Watson in her book about the first crossing. "Channel swimming is about oneself, and crossing the Channel is never less than a rite of passage in the swimmer's life." A California physicist who swam it in 1988 elaborated. "The sea is not suscep-tible to human vanity," observed David Clark. "When I got out of the ocean, stood on the shoreline in France and looked back across the Channel, it did not look defeated to me. What we conquer are our own limitations."

That's also why Diana Nyad chose the treacherous course from Havana to Key West, 103 miles of open water that could take sixty hours to cross. "I wasn't searching for some grand accomplishment to do," she said. "I was just thinking, how to live my everyday life so I don't have any regrets at the end?" At sixty-one she was swim-ming for anyone who has ever agonized that growing older means saying good-bye to dreams. Months before the event, I meet her in Manhattan to find out about her mindset and her training. At 8 AM she's already done two and a half hours of fifty-yard laps at a steady sixty strokes per minute. That's both arms every second, nonstop.

Watching her swim is unnerving. When we go across the street for breakfast, she is ravenous. Oatmeal, yogurt, berries, bananas, eggs, bacon. Watching her eat is encouraging. "I don't feel old," she tells me. "Yeah, I'm a bit slower than I was, burlier. But I'm pretty darn strong. Used to be like a racehorse—now I'm more like a Clydesdale." One with more than a little horse sense about the mystical qualities of long-distance swimming.

"People save up their whole lives to go to Nepal to sit in an ashram," she says. "They just want to go where I'm going—to get out of their daily lives and explore the universe of their mind."

In the summer of 2011 she made her fourth attempt at what became a much-publicized swim. Partway across, two deadly jellyfish—the Portuguese man-of-war—whipped their long, stringy tentacles, injecting lethal toxins into her body. "It was as if a science fiction whisk flew across my body in less than 1/1000th of a second," Nyad later wrote. "The pain is excruciating. Intolerable. As if you have been held down in boiling oil. I yelled out FIRE, FIRE, I'M ON FIRE!!" As the paralysis from the venom spread, she had trouble breathing; her life was in danger. She finally agreed to quit, her dream crushed. "We plan for one scenario, one relationship . . . and a very different animal presents itself," she concluded, after her body healed. "And we survive."

That calm acceptance of the inevitable unites many of the open-water swimmers I meet, a lesson that goes beyond any body of water.

"You don't conquer Mother Nature," explains my pool pal Alan Morrison, a robust lawyer with enviable shoulder muscles whose long-distance swims include the Santa Barbara Channel, Boston Harbor, and Tampa Bay. "I don't swim marathons to win. It's to have a long visit and hope that Mother Nature lets me through." Sometimes she doesn't. "My first long swim was around Key West in 2006," he recalls. "A squall came up, and the lightning started. That crackly kind of lightning. Then the safety boat came by, and the guy said, 'We strongly urge you to get in the boat.' I was on board before he finished the sentence."

Alan is an attorney specializing in biotechnology and pharmaceutical law, which may help explain his affinity for water. "Swimming is a fabulous sport for anything quantitative," he explains over breakfast one morning after a workout, "because you're always counting. In the pool it's always a math exercise; it's pattern recognition, formation." During the marathon, it's just plain grit. "There are parts that are pure hell," he answers, when I ask about the fourteen-hour, twenty-four-mile Tampa Bay swim he has just completed. "In the middle you're reevaluating everything. You consider canceling the other two you've already signed up for. You start getting melancholy. You really start wishing you had died as a child." I'm not sure he's joking. "Then," he recalls, "I thought, 'If I represented myself as an attorney, what would it take to quit? What excuse would be compelling enough?' Then, 'how would I feel when I woke up the next morning?' That stopped me. I just kept telling myself, 'It's kind of like your Bar Mitzvah. You can't quit! Half the planet's watching on the Internet.'" Which is where he's met many of them. He took up swimming as an adult, he says, and "it's changed my life. Of all the people I know on Facebook, almost all wear swim caps."

That's another common refrain among swimmers today: the loneliness of the long-distance swimmer has been supplanted by the digital and daily support of colleagues, as group swims and more social open-water challenges have become more available. You still can't chat when your head is underwater, and it's unlikely that the boss will organize a foursome for a swim outing, but like the transformation of the backyard pool to an outdoor living room, swimming is emphasizing the communal as much as the competitive. There are open-water events from South Africa to Sweden;

The race is called "Escape from Alcatraz." The water is cold.

in the United States, from Chesapeake Bay to Alcatraz Island. Open water became an Olympic event in 2008 in Beijing. In 2012 it will be a ten-kilometer (six-mile) race in London's Serpentine, a lake in the middle of Hyde Park with a storied racing past, including Christmas Day plunges into its iced-over waters, often requiring a hatchet.

In New York, more than 2,100 swimmers participated in fourteen major events run by NYC Swim last summer, from a car-free crossing

under the Brooklyn Bridge to the circumlocution of the Statue of Liberty to the killer 17.5-mile marathon called the Ederle Swim, after Gertrude, who first freestyled from lower Manhattan to Sandy Hook, New Jersey, in 1925. The signature swim is the 28.5-mile trip around Manhattan Island, inspired by Diana Nyad's record-breaking excursion in 1975. "I breathed to the left, and swimming counterclockwise I saw New York all day," she tells me long after the fact. "And people took off work or came down for a few hours and cheered me on. I looked down the expanse of the Hudson and went under the George

From Brooklyn to Manhattan without the bridge—NYC Swim 2010

Washington Bridge and could see the Statue of Liberty all the way down. It was magnificent." That special view of the world's most special city was also described by Dave Tanner, now coaching high school swimmers in Indiana. "I swam along the East River," he tells me. "I saw the United Nations. I passed taxis—I was going faster than they were. Then I headed down the Hudson. It took seven and a half hours. My shoulders were so sore, I couldn't shift the gears driving home. My friend shifted from the passenger seat!"

Morty Berger, a banker and swimmer, started NYC Swim to revive an activity that once permeated the Big Apple. "This is a second dance for the sport," he tells me, citing the glory years when match races and endurance swims by Ederle and a pack of predecessors made regular runs in the city's waterways. He says the momentum has been building, thanks to the quadrennial buzz about the Olympics, the aging of a population that cannot do marathons and triathlons forever, and the more-than-admirable cleanup of the

Encircling Lady Liberty with NYC Swim 2010

city's waters. "It's a perfect storm now, because there's a little edge of danger as well," Berger says. "You know, darker water, Jaws is gonna get you."

He's only partly kidding. "There's a kind of magic when you're out there, in your zone," Berger goes on. "It allows you to have your own private thrill." Which is as poetic as he gets. I ask what makes swimming special. "Some say it's the womb, but I don't remember that and don't wish to revisit it even with a psychiatrist."

Berger's biggest booster and volunteer public ambassador doesn't need any outside help. "Swimming is my drug, my therapy, my church," says Capri Djatiasmoro, sixty, a bubbly self-described mermaid whose enthusiasm has ushered many into New York's waters. Almost any weekend, year-round, you can find her at the beach—in a black Speedo with a snappy camera tucked into the bodice. "My cleavage cam," she explains, sneaking in a quick shot that will later be posted online. Capri works in advertising, coordinating outdoor

Close Encounters of the Aquatic Kind

Five hours into his marathon swim across Tampa Bay, Alan Morrison felt fish nibbling at his thighs. "Actually, they were pressing their bodies against me and vibrating," he recalls. "I didn't know if they were trying to mate with me and this was foreplay." They continued to vibrate as they moved down his legs. After five or ten seconds, they'd go away, then return after five or ten minutes. There were at least ten encounters. The first time he stopped abruptly and told the woman kayaking alongside, 'Something is crawling down my leg.' She smiled. I asked if I had anything to worry about. She said no. So I swam on."

As a child, Capri Djatiasmoro often swam alone in the Caribbean waters off Mexico. Calmly and soberly, she tells me, "Once I ran into this five-foot barracuda. We both scared the shit out of each other! I know that he freaked out because his colors changed, from cool silver to blotchy gray. So mentally I was thinking, and talking to the barracuda, and I said, 'Listen, I understand this is your territory, but I'm just passing through. I mean you no harm.' So then he calmed down, and he said, 'OK, but you scared me!' I said, 'You know, you scared me! But just let me pass, 'cause I'm just passing through.' And that was that." I ask if the dialogue was all in her head. "Well, I think we were communicating," she replies. And then she starts to tell me about the time she was scuba diving and heard a noise like a rattlesnake, then saw lobster claws on a ledge. "And lobsters are very curious. So I waved, and he felt the wave and came out, and calmed down. Fish are just like people," she explains. "They have personalities."

national campaigns for major corporations. But her heart remains in the water. "I wish I could swim all the time," she says to me one evening over dinner. "I always complain at the office, 'I'm missing a really great beach day. And if you really appreciate me, I want a waterproof laptop that I could take to the beach!'" A former triathlete with the musculature to match, she has completed almost every event sponsored by NYC Swim and gets depressed if she goes more than a week out of the water. "It's very calming," she tells me. "As soon as I get into the water, all the mental garbage, all the internal chatter"—moving her fingers around her head like a tightly wound spring—"all that stuff goes away. Especially with long-distance swims. I check my form; then I go wandering around the universe."

The camaraderie among swimmers, particularly in open water, is contagious. My Hellespont swim was preceded by a round of parties and meetings that produced instant friendships and mutual support. And that's just one of the events organized by SwimTrek, which bills itself as "the world's leading swimming holiday operator." (There are at least half a dozen others I found around the world.) In 2003, when it began, they took just under 100 swimmers to three spots. In 2011, they took more than 2,000 people to twenty-six locations, including Greece, Croatia, and Egypt. That partly reflects "more awareness of the great outdoors," says founder Simon Murie. "Thirty years ago, inland waterways and lakes were considered trash areas, where you put your pollution. Now they're cleaner than they've ever been, and people realize that there's more to do than swim in a pool."

No one has explored the human potential of the oceans better than Lynne Cox, the gifted swimmer and eloquent writer who has helped change the face of swimming in the wild. Her generosity to other swimmers is legendary; her passion for the earth's waters, unbounded. "I'll open up an atlas and see all the blue places," she explains, "but each is different—in color, taste, buoyancy. Each is a world in itself." With two record English Channel crossings (the first before she was old enough to drive) and a string of other global successes, she has reclaimed the oceans as avenues for swimmers. "You are lifted by the waves," she tells me. "Everything is always changing, even the light on the water. The different kinds of froth. And at night, the phosphorous sparks fly." What she really appreciates is "knowing you're part of something else."

Lynne is best known for her ice-water swims, bone-piercing immersions, which she partly attributes to the wet suit she's grown on her body. "If I were a tall, lean guy, I wouldn't get far in the water," she says matter-of-factly. "No body fat." Her internal temperature is 1 degree cooler than average, and yes, that makes a difference. The lower baseline means she doesn't have to work as hard to keep it warm. She can also voluntarily close down her peripheral blood flow "so it migrates to my core." She sweats in a 76-degree pool. But in the unimaginably frigid waters where she's swum—the Bering Sea, the Antarctic, Alaska's Glacier Bay—she does indeed feel the cold. She just doesn't focus on it. "You don't want to give energy to it," she says, another life lesson from the blue.

Great advice, but not the sort of thing I'd try at home. I've always like my water, well, warm. Not hot. Okay, cool. But not cold. That is to say, I am happiest when there is no shock to the system, which means little discernable difference between the warmth of the air and that of the liquid I'm entering. Except for certain killer scorching days, I like to slide into a friendly, womb-like world. It is safe. It is

Winter bathing caps for Coney Island Polar Bears

comforting. I am, however, getting more flexible as a result of my Hellespont training. I've discovered that colder (translation: very *slightly* cooler) water is better for faster swims and longer workouts. A quick chill can be energizing. But I know my limits.

One brisk Sunday morning in February, I head out to see the Coney Island Polar Bears—not a group of Arctic animals, but a collection of sturdy souls who choose to take a dip when the temperature takes a dive. Polar Bear clubs exist all over the country, many daring only on New Year's Day to bathe in frigid water, usually to raise money for charity. The Coney Island Polar Bear Club calls itself the oldest in the United States, and they swim in the Atlantic Ocean every single Sunday from November through April. After clomping

That's snow, not sand.

through a field of snow to get to the bleak wintry beach, I find a dozen or so Bears—including retirees, freelancers, a postal worker, and a pastry chef—casually milling about in the 46-degree sunshine. It is just after noon, and I am wearing jeans, a turtleneck, a parka, boots, gloves, and a scarf tied snugly around my neck. They are all dressed or, rather, undressed, in bikinis or boxers over both beer bellies and trim bodies. No one is shivering.

"You can't be more democratic than in a bathing suit," says one member, laughing. "Every day is a beach day," explains another, a tall, thin fellow who came on doctor's orders twenty-one years ago to get some exercise in winter. "The first time it felt like pins and needles, but then it clicked." Louis Padilla, sixty-nine, used to operate an elevator in Manhattan's garment center. He also used to need

Yes, those are snowflakes. Big ones.

crutches because "my knees were gone—I couldn't walk straight." After twenty-seven years of swimming here, "it all disappeared. No pain. I love it. It's cold, but I don't feel it so much." The health thing comes up a lot with the Polar Bears, because their founder, back in 1903, advocated physical fitness long before it was popular. Cold water was part of the mix. And remains the lure. "It's crazy and fun and cheaper than therapy," adds Bob Croce, fifty-one, who did his first cold-water dunk on a dare. "It's about those endorphins." I ask how he warms up after the swim. "At the end? I just run to the car," he says, laughing.

Just after 1 PM, club president Dennis Thomas, fifty-five, leads the Bears through the snow and down to the beach. I join the march with a bald sushi chef who remembers the time he swam in Lake

George, "when I had hair, and when I came up from the water all my hair was frozen"; with Mike Spataro, a strapping ex-marine who drives here weekly from his home in New Jersey. "It takes me one hour and two bridges," he says proudly. "And it's expensive, too." Mike starts to laugh as he recalls the day they swam through a blinding blizzard, a moment captured in a hilarious video that I later see online, and another day when the windchill factor brought the temperature down to about 10 degrees. "The sand was like razors; we backed into the water." Today he's barefoot.

Then Dennis Thomas launches into the weekly ritual: the swimmers form a big circle, where he leads them in a chant—today it's about the Super Bowl—accompanied by blood-warming jumping jacks. That sends them into the water, just above freezing, where they bravely form another circle, hooting loudly, then swim off at will. One woman in a green cap takes off as if it's summer. A slender young woman wearing a fake fur hat and a tiger print bikini retreats to the beach almost immediately, the bright pink skin two inches above her studded navel marking how far she stepped in. "That's all I can take," says Adrienne Adams, a private caterer, shivering. So why wear a bikini? "The suit wouldn't have made a difference." As one of the regulars, she does it, I assume, from a deep if loony desire to embrace the chill. I am dead wrong. "I hate winter," she tells me, her pink skin now turning blue. "This is my surrender. This is just my way to deal with it."

In all, they swim about twelve minutes. Capri Djatiasmoro is here, casually shaking off the winter water. "This just feels great—you should try it!" she insists. "Within two minutes, you release a chemical cocktail—dopamine, serotonin, endorphins. That's the Polar Bear high." From my totally dry and warm spot on the beach, I ask how cold it felt. "You know when you're at a party, and you put your arm into the bucket of ice to get the last beer? That's how cold it is.

Red Tide

The photo looked fake: one little head bobbing among 5,000 in a mass swimathon across China's Yangtze River in July 1966. But Mao Zedong was indeed there, a stroke of political theater to dispel rumors that the enigmatic chairman, seventy-two, was ill and unfit to lead. A lifelong swimmer ("Do you swim? Water is a good thing"), he showed up in Wuhan unannounced and executed his peculiar "lounge-chair style"—on his back, arms and legs adrift—to float some nine miles downstream for more than an hour. The current was as favorable as the reception. He even paused to teach the backstroke to a young girl. The crowd, reported the state-run media, erupted into "spasms of cheers." The outside world read the aquatic tea leaf as a sign that Chairman Mao was prepared to resume control of the tumultuous Cultural Revolution. Chinese citizens saw it as an invitation to follow the Great Leader through the changing tides of power. "There was old Mao waving his hand," said one, recalling the picture of him wrapped in his bathrobe. "He may as well have been standing on the water."

紧跟伟大领袖毛主席在大风大浪中奋勇前进

The poster reads, in part, "Closely follow the great leader Chairman Mao and forge ahead courageously amid great storms and waves."

On your whole body. It's a shock, but so in the moment. Nothing else exists. You are right there dealing with it. Right there." She is smiling—they all are—and it actually (am I crazy?) looks like fun. I am almost tempted to try it. Almost.

As Dennis Thomas heads back through the snow, barefoot, I ask whether he swims there in the summer as well. "Nope," he says. "Too crowded."

I'm guessing a pool wouldn't suit him either.

7

Stream
Lines

LIKE MOST SWIMMERS *from less buttoned-down eras, Leander crossed the Hellespont naked, knotting his cloak around his head before plunging in to visit his lover on the other side. When you're a myth, you can do anything. A few millennia later, Gertrude Ederle did it in real life, slipping out of her homemade silk bra while crossing the English Channel in search of comfort, not romance. Male swimmers were permitted to cross with nothing protecting their masculinity but a layer of grease. The images come to mind during my own adventure because the water feels so soft and pearly, I wouldn't mind being naked myself. It's how I prefer to swim when I'm alone, sliding through the stream minus even the barest of barriers. So primal. So impractical. So I've thought carefully about what suit to bring from my very well-stocked collection: a strapless number that frees my shoulders and makes me feel like Esther Williams? A two-piece halter-top that might let me do an Ederle to get up close and personal with the Hellespont? A soft little bandeau with sequins (body bling; I like glitter) on the front? In the interest of propriety and pace, I've settled on a speed suit—purple, so I'd know it was me. While the unforgiving second skin won't hide the kebabs I've consumed since arriving in Turkey, it won't slow me down or chafe me, either. Better yet, I got it online, without ever having to go to a dressing room.*

Want to see a grown woman—any woman—act like the victim in a horror film? Two words: bathing suit. Three more: trying one on. "I think the day you go to buy a bathing suit is the day that even women who like to shop feel like committing suicide," says Nora Ephron, coauthor of the play *Loss, Loss and What I Wore,* which X-rays our feelings about clothing. Calling swimsuits clothing may be charitable. "Underwear," proclaims Patricia Marx drily in the *New Yorker.* But "unlike underwear, they do not work behind the scenes. Bathing suits are the whole show." Worse yet, she writes, "You know who looks fabulous in a bathing suit? A mannequin. Also, a hanger."

Marx, who is trim enough not to worry, swam laps naked while a student at Harvard because, she says, "I was presexual. I assumed everyone was there just to swim. No one was looking." Years later she mentioned that to a male college friend, who said incredulously, "Are you kidding? Why do you think I was a lifeguard?"

At least he was more appreciative than the unforgiving fluorescents of the fitting room. One glimpse at the three-way mirror under the ghastly glare, and you recognize pores you haven't seen since senior prom, wrinkles you're paying Estée Lauder to hide. Speaking personally, my skin is fish-belly white. And belly fat from three directions is at least two too many. Wait. That's back fat. Most women I know would rather expose themselves to the media and run for president than bare their bodies in Bloomingdale's. One who has done both understands the gravity of the problem. In an environmental speech to high-tech executives during her 2007 campaign, Hillary Rodham Clinton acknowledged that replacing incandescent light bulbs with more energy-efficient CFRs was stalled by the bulbs' sickly shade of green. "Every woman in this audience knows what it is like to try on a bathing suit in a dressing room with a fluorescent light," said the then senator, instantly earning the vote of fashion victims nationwide. "There will not be broad-based market acceptance until we get a better glow!" For columnist Ellen Goodman, the solution is simple: replace the fluorescents (in the dressing rooms, not eco-friendly American homes) with candles, and mandate only one long skinny mirror. And we all live happily ever after in the land of size 2.

Until then, there is spandex. Pull it out—it snaps back; tug it over your bulges—it mashes them flat. Spandex is an anagram for "expands," which it does, then recoils to make sure you don't. It does for swimmers what months of sit-ups have not. "We were the first to use it," recalls Miriam Ruzow, who designed the ultrachic suits for her family-run Gottex brand, which compacted the bodies of bathers from Elizabeth Taylor to Princess Di. "The bigger amounts we used, the more it controlled," she says. "And the prints were like a camouflage. We knew what to highlight and what to cover up."

Today's spandex queen is Miraclesuit. "If she has a little bit of a tummy, it flattens it; a little bit of a rear, it lifts; if her bodice area is a little bit lacking or overzealous, it compensates." Sandra Davidoff, director of corporate relations for Miraclesuit, is telling me about the phenomenally successful line of stylish swimwear that promises to make women "look 10 lbs. lighter in 10 seconds." "It's the best compression suit out there," she says, denying any comparison to sausage casing. "Nothing pops out of any spot where it shouldn't be. It just sucks you in and keeps you in." Miraclesuit's secret is a triple dose of nylon Lycra (brand name for spandex) for "triple the holding power," Davidoff explains. "A yard of fabric that's protecting our bodies against the world." I think about the heavy, boned girdles of another era, which condensed my mother the way *Reader's Digest* condensed books. Only the fibers have changed. "Most women have body issues," Davidoff says. "Nobody thinks she's good enough to strut her stuff. You want to be able to walk to the beach or the pool and feel confident that everything stays where it belongs, that nothing is jiggling."

The market is confirmed by Miraclesuit's consumers. The largest size in the line, which used to be 18, is now 24W—a sign of the corpulent times in which we are living, Davidoff explains. Even Speedo, the least you can wear for fast, efficient swimming, has seen its most popular size grow from a 10 to a 14. "But there's another side to it," explains Kate Wilton, Speedo's director of performance. "People who aren't as fit still want to get into the water and exercise." And there are suits for them.

Speedo, which helped lead the revolution from wool to nylon to Lycra, now uses its own version of "extra-life Lycra" to "inspire aquatic confidence," Wilton says. "We want swimmers of all levels to get into the water. We want to make swimming a sport for everyone." Its signature model is the shoulder-baring Ultraback, an X-shaped backstrap that "doesn't move around when you swim laps. You don't want your straps to slip off." Ultrabacks frame the bulging lats propelling swimmers down pool lanes across America. What you see when they turn over is less inspiring. Call it the uni-bosom. "Yes, it's just smooshing everything down," Wilton agrees. "We've found that it's easier to swim through the water if you're more compressed, almost like a sports bra with running. Not the most flattering thing to wear, but it helps you exercise more efficiently. Our suits are for performance."

At Aqualab in England, Speedo's top-secret research and development facility, scientists investigate how the anti-drag properties in everything from jet planes to Formula One cars can be applied to speed suits, using high-speed underwater video to observe how water moves over a swimmer's body. The current gold standard, worn by top racers, is a lightweight, woven (the others are knit) fabric that feels like paper and conforms to the body, if you can imagine, even more like a second skin than your basic Ultraback. "Don't try it on," Wilton warns me about the wispy sample she lets me fondle. "It would take you a really long time to get into it. They are so tight and so compressive, the first time someone puts one on usually takes up to twenty minutes. It's a lot of work." Surprisingly, even the superbly toned torsos on Olympians need some help. Wilton says tiny waists are a hindrance because "when you dive in, water would get stuck in your waist and slow you down when it hit the hips. So we try to compress the body front to back to make a flat surface, filling in the waist so it's the same width as the hips. That way, water flows over the body as quickly as possible." And up front? "Yes, it drastically reduces the size of the chest. We're trying to make as few bumps and grooves in the body as possible."

But Speedo and other manufacturers had their own bumpy ride with aerodynamically accurate creations that may have rocketed athletes right to the wall. It's now called the Suit Era—the years from 2000 to 2009, when polyurethane body clingers that looked like high-tech versions of what my grandfather wore in winter helped swimmers smash some two hundred records in more-than-record time. Fans loved the speed, the excitement of seeing hundredths of seconds shaved off by a skin. Critics charged that the suits, for both men and women, were performance-enhancing, adding buoyancy and improving the flight to the finish line. In 2009 FINA, the sport's official organizing body, outlawed them, banning polyurethane from the pool and setting up new rules. Official competitive swimmers must now wear suits that are woven, knitted, or braided from fabric—that is, no more of those better-living-through-chemistry costumes. We have entered the Textile Era (yes, it's really called that), with rules that specify how much of the body can be covered (knees to waist for males, knees to shoulders for females), how thick the fabric must be (to prevent buoyancy that would aid flotation), and that it must have no zippers or—ready for this?—scales. No fish need apply.

Speedo's solution for 2012 is a compression suit with zones of a newly patented Lycra, compacting buttocks, chest, and legs for women; just the bottom half for men. It's part of a first-ever completely coordinated racing ensemble—cap (molded more like a human head than a moon), goggles (double-sealed, cat's eye sleek), and suit—called the Fastskin³, engineered, according to Aqualab's Dr. Tom Waller, so that water flows unobstructed over the racer's body. "The cap hands the flow off to the goggles so that there's no

Tip to toe flow around Michael Phelps in the 2012 Speedo

point where water can escape," he says, all the way down the body. "Water follows from the tips of the fingers to the tips of the toes." The result: a 5.2 percent reduction in active drag, claims Dr. Waller. At the rollout for the new suits, Speedo USA president Jim Gerson eyes the Olympians modeling the outfits and says, with approval, "How scary they all look!" Freestyle champion Ryan Lochte adds this threat to the competition in London: "When I put it on I feel like a super hero, an action figure, ready to take on the world!"

Natalie Coughlin in Fastskin[3]

That racers prefer the modified long-john look in an industry previously sprinting toward minimalism is ironic indeed. The narrative of modern swimwear is the story of less—from bloomers to bikinis for women, from baggy trousers to banana hammocks (ask a kid) for men. But the battle to liberate human flesh from the confines of Victorian prudery was frustrating. Female bathers had to wear fabrics and styles more suitable for church: gray flannel trousers and sleeves to the wrist; full skirts topped by sailor blouses and puffy sleeves made of black serge or mohair.

The prim "fashion for concealment," wrote one observer of the "much-clothing craze" in 1905, was not healthy. "Especially in the United States, no monstrous disfigurement that can by any means be flaunted on land seems too grotesque for women in the water.

Full coverage at the beach, 1895

Hats, shoes, even stockings, are worn at those mixed picnics for what some call bathing. . . . We shall next be told to put on clothes before getting into our baths at home, for fear of seeing our own bodies."

What Europeans, especially the French and British, did with their bodies at the seashore gives new meaning to the idea of taking a dip. In fact, they were dipped—a technical term—by "dippers," from a "bathing machine," an enclosed cubicle on wheels that carried you directly from the beach to the waves. Inside the horse-drawn chamber, a proper lady could replace her city garb with equally cumbersome bathing attire in complete if Spartan privacy; a canvas awning extended from the roof and snaked down to the water so she could slide into the sea unobserved. This sanctuary from disgrace was frequently accom-

Bathing machines at a Belgian beach, circa 1890–1900

panied by sturdy attendants (the dippers), who dunked the aquatically challenged into the brine for minutes of soothing surf. Jane Austen famously enjoyed one; so did the royal family. Men used them too, but they got to swim naked.

Bathing machines were so much more popular overseas than in the United States that when Russian diva Ida Rubenstein was invited to perform at New York's Palace Theatre in 1915, she demanded "my own little house on wheels that I may be drawn into the water where one may bathe discreetly but becomingly." Madame Rubenstein was particularly concerned lest American "prudery forbids me the one-piece bathing suit" she'd been freely wearing on the French coast.

The Bathing Machine

Imagine to yourself a small, snug, wooden chamber, fixed upon a wheel-carriage, having a door at each end, and, on each side, a little window above, a bench below. The bather, ascending into this apartment by wooden steps, shuts himself in, and begins to undress, while the attendant yokes a horse to the end next the sea, and draws the carriage forwards, till the surface of the water is on a level with the floor of the dressing-room, then he moves and fixes the horse to the other end. The person within, being stripped, opens the door to the sea-ward, where he finds the guide ready, and plunges headlong into the water. After having bathed, he reascends into the apartment, by the steps which had been shifted for that purpose, and puts on his clothes at his leisure, while the carriage is drawn back again upon the dry land; so that he has nothing further to do, but to open the door, and come down as he went up. Should he be so weak or ill as to require a servant to put off and on his clothes, there is room enough in the apartment for half-a-dozen people. The guides who attend the ladies in the water are of their own sex, and they and the female bathers have a dress of flannel for the sea; nay, they are provided with other conveniences for the support of decorum. A certain number of the machines are fitted with tilts, that project from the seaward ends of them, so as to screen the bathers from the view of all persons whatsoever. . . . The machines can be used only at a certain time of the tide, which varies every day; so that sometimes the bathers are obliged to rise very early in the morning. For my part, I love swimming as an exercise, and can enjoy it at all times of the tide, without the formality of an apparatus.
—Tobias Smollett, *The Expedition of Humphrey Clinker,* 1771

Enter Annette Kellerman. The Australian champion had been swimming for years in a unitard of her own making—sleeveless, scoop-neck, body-hugging, like a boy's racing suit—either with or without full leg stockings. It had served her well in the Yarra, Seine, and Thames, even while entertaining the queen of England. Now in America, where she'd been invited to add her mermaid act to a number of amusement parks and vaudeville shows, she took one look at the beaches and gasped, "How could these women swim with shoes—stockings—bloomers—skirts—overdresses with puffed sleeves—sailor collars—in some cases even tightly fitted corsets? But then nobody really went swimming. Everybody waded in and out and then just bobbed up and down."

The popular story, based entirely on her own account, is that she showed up at Revere Beach near Boston in 1908 and decided to go for a swim. Her bare legs immediately got the attention of a policeman, who took her to court. Her often-repeated defense ("I can't swim wearing more stuff than you hang on a clothesline") swayed the judge, who released her to swim a three-mile exercise run in Boston harbor. While the story doesn't show up in any newspaper accounts or court documents, the result is legitimate swimming history: Annette Kellerman changed forever the way women thought about dressing for and dealing with the water. That part can be easily tracked in America's dailies. The newspapers loved it—any photo of a woman in a bathing suit was the kind of legal voyeurism that safely made the front page. Still does.

Annette Kellerman and her perfect form

Kellerman says she appeased the law by agreeing to be wrapped in a robe when she was not swimming or performing. She also added tights to her knees, then tied a flimsy swatch of fabric around her waist to give the illusion she was fully dressed. Kellerman was very good at illusion. She went on to a stupendous career in vaudeville, then Hollywood, and was even named "The Perfect Woman" by a Harvard professor who decided her measurements most closely resembled those of the Venus de Milo. Her act was occasionally scandalous, often cheeky ("What we are selling here is backsides," explained the showman who added multiple mirrors to her swimming tank, "and a hundred backsides are better than one!"), but it showed women what they, too, could do.

And in an era when the police prowled the beaches with tape measures to make sure not an inch of extra epidermis was exposed, her suit started a revolution.

Taping the flesh, Washington, D.C., 1922. The distance from knee to hem had to be six inches at most.

In time, hemlines receded, liberating limbs, necks, and navels to the sun. Taboos were lifted, new lightweight fabrics were invented, and eight yards of heavy wool that shrouded women's curves shriveled to a single swath of body-hugging, synthetic smoothness that flaunted them. As sportswriter Paul Gallico wrote of An-

nette Kellerman's breakthrough swimsuit, "It made the question of how ladies were put together no longer a matter of vague speculation."

For a time, suits were gender-neutral, sporty little tank tops attached to thigh-high shorts that looked exactly like the outfits worn by men. I know because I have a yellowing photo of two spiffy dress-alikes on a New Jersey beach: my mother and father, looking dashing in those very suits.

By the late 1930s, men were allowed to dump the undershirts. And Hollywood culture steered women's suits toward less coverage, more cleavage. Betty Grable took American GIs to war with a come-hither look that forever ended the question of whether a bathing suit could be sexy from the rear. And while the end of World War II meant the end of rationing fabric, designers were in no mood to amplify. They preferred less coverage, more cleavage. And whatever else they could get away with. In 1946, just after the United States had exploded test nuclear weapons on the Pacific atoll called Bikini, Swiss engineer Louis Reard and French couturier Jacques Heim separately sewed up tiny little patches for strategic parts of the female body. There was not a lot of sewing. Someone named the skimpy new suit the bikini—perhaps because of its explosive effect on the planet. When Brigitte Bardot put it on (and took it off) in the movies,

Shirley Sherr on the beach
in New Jersey, 1920s

nobody confused it with a Speedo. The inimitable Diana Vreeland,
then at *Harper's Bazaar*, dubbed the bikini the "swoonsuit," calling it
"the most important thing since the atom bomb." She later quipped
that it revealed "everything about a girl except her mother's maiden
name." All that exposure took its toll on American women. In the
1960 song "Itsy Bitsy Teeny Weeny Yellow Polka Dot Bikini," the first-
time wearer is so embarrassed, she hides in the locker room, then
in a towel, then in the water to avoid being seen. The song, however,
soared to the top of the pop charts, a sure sign that the suit was here
to stay.

Before there was a swoosh or a polo player, the Jantzen diving girl in the corner of your bathing suit meant you were wearing the right thing.

Another generation of designs with more descriptive names soon followed: the thong, the topless, an industry of-inis. Manufacturers added stiff "bones" for structure, ruffles for fun. In time they even eliminated the modesty panel—the little strip of fabric that covered the crotch so that, well, the crotch would be covered. But the relaxation of morals also stripped away the same attitudes that had kept so many women out of the water.

In 1917 a courtroom stenographer named Charlotte Epstein, who enjoyed swimming after work, founded the Women's Swimming Association in New York, the first such club organized in America to train champion swimmers. Epstein then convinced the Amateur Athletic Union to allow women to compete: another first. And to make them faster—which meant losing the leggings that had become de rigueur with the Kellerman suit—Epstein arranged for two of her stars, Ethelda Bleibtry and Charlotte Boyle, to show up at a Brooklyn beach without stockings. They were, as planned, arrested for "nude swimming," but the publicity and public outcry decided the case. The girls were released from jail and from wearing stockings forever more. Epstein was ingenious. In those years before women got the right to vote, she also arranged suffrage swims to raise money for the cause. And in 1920 she helped negotiate the participation of America's first female swimmers in the Olympic games—eight years after the USOC allowed them in. She also managed the team. Six years later, Epstein selected another of her stars to swim the English Channel. Her name was Gertrude Ederle. American women were in the water for good.

It was a far cry from the dainty image of earlier times. Theodore Roosevelt, one of our swimming presidents, once stripped down for a dip in the Potomac with a group of personal and governmental friends. Someone pointed out to the French ambassador that he hadn't removed his gloves. "I think I will leave them on," he responded ever so Gallically. "We might meet ladies!"

What you wear in the water depends on your needs, but everyone definitely needs goggles. Largely unknown until the 1970s—Olympians weren't even allowed to wear them until 1976—they have revolutionized swimmers' wardrobes the way seat belts have changed the way we ride in automobiles: you just don't go in without them. Racers prefer tiny, hard plastic lenses strapped as close to the face as possible. Racers also suffer more silently than the rest of us. One former freestyler tells me she just lived with the pain when the tight pair that fit into her eye socket left a calcium deposit in her browline. Think migraine. I spent years seeking the perfect pair of goggles: Some leaked. Some made me feel penned in. They all hurt and left deep rings around my eyes. I thought I'd figured it out with a comfy brand that rested gently on foam, but they only fit erratically. I have finally found true goggle contentment with a slightly larger style from Aqua Sphere that allows me a more panoramic view and doesn't leave me looking like a raccoon.

Sometimes a Suit Won't Help

In the *Seinfeld* episode called "The Hamptons," George is changing after a dip in the swimming pool when Jerry's girlfriend accidentally walks into the room and sees him naked. *Gasp!* As her eyes slide south, she giggles and apologizes, not at all convincingly. Then bolts from the room, still chuckling. George inspects himself and screams in frustration. Women, it seems, don't understand the science of shrinkage. It's all about cold water.

When the frigid sea and a strong north wind thwarted Byron's first attempt to cross the Hellespont, he wondered whether "Leander's conjugal affection must not have been chilled in his passage to paradise." And the Coney Island Polar Bears have been known to chant this before they hit the icy Atlantic: "Shrinkage comes and shrinkage goes; Monday morning no one knows." They were not quoting Byron.

Fins are shorter than flippers and can be very useful to strengthen the legs. And then there is music, or whatever else you'd like to hear. Recently, in the interest of multitasking, I purchased a waterproof case for my smallest iPod and plugged into a series of audio books while lapping back and forth in the pool. The listening was fine—I chose mostly novels about ancient history, to keep me above the daily grind—but the earplugs never quite fit right, and the wires connected to the case on my upper arm shattered the illusion of myself-as-mermaid. I decided to abandon it until I run out of things to think about.

Speaking of which, I've solved the problem of keeping track of my laps—frustratingly elusive when you're dreaming big dreams—with a nifty little finger ring called the SportCount Chrono 100. You thumb down a button when you hit the wall, and it tallies your lengths (and minutes) electronically. It is endlessly practical. "Some Buddhists and Hare Krishnas count their prayers with them," says Bernard Fitzmorris, a practicing dentist from Washington, D.C., who invented the gadget when he kept forgetting what lap he was on. "We also get notes about women timing their contractions when they're in labor. And there's a bungee club that ordered a bunch to see how long each bounce lasts."

But for all the new tools to make our inner swimmer more comfortable, no one has figured out hair. Chlorine strips its color and luster. Latex crushes the follicles and makes you look downright ugly. Is there no hope for swim caps? You'd think that a nation that got us to the moon, etc. You'd think they could actually make one that's attractive. You would be wrong.

The problem is, caps are not designed to keep your hair dry. They're about keeping hair out of the drains of pools and about keeping you streamlined. For guys too. That they make us look like the pin-headed taste buds from the old TV commercials is just plain dumb. Surely there are better solutions.

Esther Williams made it look easy with a smile that never melted and hair that never wavered in the waves. But her arrangements are impractical. She wore special cream makeup topped with powder, set in a shower. Her hair was slathered with a concoction of warm baby oil and Vaseline "that looked suitable for lubricating cars," then woven into braids, topped by artificial braids pinned up to stay put. By "the time I came out of hair and makeup," she writes, "I was as waterproof as a mallard."

For many African American women, hair has been the showstopper. "A lot of black people raised the way I was—in cities, which is most of us—don't like the water," says Josie, the swimming protagonist in Martha Southgate's novel *The Taste of Salt*. The reasons: "hair, money, time, lack of opportunity." Mostly hair. Josie solves the problem by cutting off her cornrows to "let my head be free. . . . I'm never growing it back." Southgate did the same, but she's unusual.

Tracy Roach was a competitive swimmer from fifth to ninth grades, a champion in butterfly and free at her school in Fort Lauderdale, Florida. "My parents were so proud when I won my medals," she remembers. But when she moved up to high school, she quit. "You get into your fashion and your clothes. And I said, I can't do that any more! So I stopped swimming and started playing volleyball." What she meant was she couldn't get her hair wet any more. Still doesn't. Like many African American women, she stays out of the water because it wrecks the hair she's so laboriously straightened. The process takes two to three hours, she says. And while her young son and daughter swim ("Curly is in now, so it's not a problem for her"), she stays out. Why not go curly herself? "No! It's too humid here," she says, accurately describing the Laundromat climate of her home state. And if her kids want to go to the beach and she just got

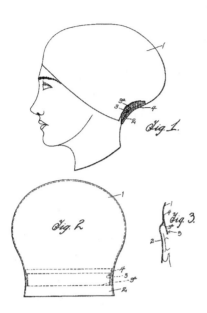

Anna Baldwin's 1922 patent for a bathing cap with a double seal and flap to "effectively exclude moisture." No known products like it exist.

her hair done? "We won't go." I try again: Can't you keep your head out of the water? "It won't work, because then you start liking it and then you go under."

For Tracy Roach, commission assistant in the City of Fort Lauderdale, swimming still tugs at her heart. "I love the water; I really do," she says, reflecting. "It's refreshing, relaxing. You're at peace. If I could swim every day and not have to worry about my hair, that would be. . . ."

A really big moneymaker.

8

Sink
or Swim

"YOU'RE GOING TO SWIM *across a body of water where someone drowned?*
That's what this is about?" A friend back home—not someone steeped in Greek
mythology—is asking, and I'm tempted to throw up my hands and conclude that some
people just don't get it. Then I realize that it's a very smart question. Why did Leander
drown in the Hellespont? He was, after all, a capable swimmer who, as Ovid imagined
him, confidently stroked his way to Hero night after night, despite the distance:

> Then, both my arms growing weary, at the shoulder,
> I raised myself strongly, high above the waves . . .
> And sudden strength returned to my weary arms,
> And the waves seemed calmer to me.
> Love aids me, warming my eager heart . . .
> I am more vigorous and the shore comes nearer . . .

Until it didn't. Some interpret Leander's death as a sign from the gods, a cautionary
tale for humans not to upset the cosmic order, not to offend divine authority. Or perhaps

it's just the peril of forbidden romance, fated from the start to end badly. Others see it as the conflict of the continents, the ongoing struggle between East and West. And then there's the fellow from our Curaçao swim camp who, on hearing the story, concludes with twenty-first-century moxie that the meaning is clear: Don't swim at night. And certainly not alone.

Excellent advice, which I am happily following on this golden afternoon in a sea full of swimmers, mindful that the tranquil channel we are traversing has the power to turn violent in a New York swimmer's minute.

"Anybody that's not afraid of the water is a fool," Ernie Burgess is telling me. "You've got to have a lot of respect for it. You've got to know how easy it is to drown." Burgess has been a lobsterman in Maine for fifty-eight (of his sixty-eight) years. Lobsterboy at first, I guess. I've asked him why so many people whose livelihood is fished out of the sea don't know how to swim. "It's true," he goes on, bemused by a question he says he's never considered. "But I have no idea why— whether it's a fatalistic attitude or because they didn't learn when they were little kids or what." He chuckles—not at the serious subject, but at the way of life for a third-generation lobsterman. "Well, I can swim. Not very well, but I can probably keep myself afloat for three to four minutes, and that's about all you've got anyway." He means because the water's so cold. A number of his friends have drowned. And he's pulled seven people out himself. But Burgess, who spends all day on the water running eight hundred lobster traps in and around Chebeague Island, doesn't swim for fun. Even in the summer, when it warms up, you won't find the lobstermen of Maine practicing their breaststroke. "We spend so much time trying to stay out of the water, that's the last thing you think about," he says. "'Cause if you're getting in, chances are the circumstances aren't gonna be too rosy!"

In 2008, accidental drownings took the lives of 4,058 people in the United States—more than ten a day. The highest rates were

Cullen Jones makes a splash in Shreveport, Louisiana

among children from ages one to four; African Americans from five to fourteen were particularly vulnerable. According to a recent study, 60 percent of minority children cannot swim, compared to 40 percent of white children. And the rate of drowning among minorities is at least three times that of white children.

Olympian Cullen Jones, who won two gold medals in Beijing, nearly drowned as a child, a terrifying experience at a water park where he was submerged for about a minute. Learning to swim changed his life. Today he tours the country for Make a Splash, the organization started by the USA Swimming Foundation to get more minority children past cultural stereotyping and into the water. On the day I meet up with Jones at an elementary school in Manhattan's Greenwich Village, he plays to the crowd of eager faces by asking what they think of a Speedo bathing suit. "Tighty-whiteys," answers one youngster, giggling. Then Jones slips off his shiny black Nike sneakers and tells the kids he got them for free. "Swimming got me shoes," he says. Whatever works. Others have proposed starting with better facilities and educational outreach in minority communities. Either way, at least one study shows that swimming lessons can reduce fatalities by 88 percent. In some countries, like Holland, where the canals weave through every city, swimming is mandatory for children.

Swim School

Earning a Harvard degree has always been demanding. It also used to demand a swimming test. But the concern for students' safety nearly sidetracked a political campaign in 1972. Senior Pat Caddell, moonlighting as the pollster for Democratic presidential nominee George McGovern, was in California for the crucial June primary when he got a call from his college roommate. The dean's office had called, and Caddell wasn't going to graduate at the ceremony two weeks hence. He'd forgotten to take his swimming test. "This causes a panic," Caddell later recalls. Luckily, the campaign contains enough creative egos to pull him through. He will take his test in the rooftop pool of the Wilshire Hyatt House in Los Angeles. And his coach will be the Gonzo journalist Hunter S. Thompson, on the trail for *Rolling Stone*. "He comes out wearing a Grateful Dead T-Shirt with a whistle," Caddell says. Along with two Pulitzer Prize–winners (Washington *Post* columnist Mary McGrory and author Theodore H. White) and a pack of journalist witnesses. "And I'm trying to swim," Caddell remembers. "And they're all talking and making bets. And Hunter is there screaming at me. I'm almost drowning, I'm laughing so hard." The swim gods are smiling too. Caddell passes and celebrates at a champagne lunch. Today he swims with his grandchildren. Harvard no longer requires the test.

Fear of the water and ineptitude in the pool may be deeply rooted, theorizes one New York psychiatrist. "You can frequently tell where someone is stuck developmentally by what they can't do in swimming," he says. "People who can't float often have trust and intimacy issues. For some, if they're arrested in development, they hold on to the side of the pool, or can't let their feet leave the bottom. It's an aquatic version of apron strings: they can't take chances." And it can affect beginners as well as good swimmers. "Putting your face in the water may have to do with the feeling that you won't be able to control what comes in. Turning your head to breathe is working without a net. It's all the same fear: that a rug will be pulled out from underneath you."

The poet Shelley never did learn and drowned at sea. But lessons aren't the only solution. You can drown in a bathtub. You can get in over your head. Bad things can happen to good swimmers. Eight years after his triumph at the English Channel, Matthew Webb found himself in financial difficulties and, in a desperate attempt at publicity, announced that he would swim the treacherous Niagara River, just below the falls. He was last seen swirling through its rapids, just ahead of the churning whirlpool; his body was found four days later, crushed by the weight of the water.

And it's not just turbulence. Former Texas coach George Block worries about water quality and temperature in the rapidly mushrooming open-water races around the world. "Suddenly kids who are world-class athletes were sick all the time, and that just scared me to death," he explains. "Especially the age group I was coaching. We were taking minor females of reproductive age and exposing them to I don't know what in the way of chemical or biological contaminants. So I feel like we should take a time out from open-water races until we deal with these issues. But there's money and Olympic medals and national prestige at stake." He mentions Dubai, where the widely respected marathoner Fran Crippen died during a race in 2010. "The issue there was the water was too hot. Now that's easily measured. I'm worried about other places where you can't measure it. And the long-term effects we don't know about yet."

Responsible race organizers like Morty Berger of NYC Swim carefully monitor everything from the tides to the temperature to the amount of flotsam and jetsam along swimmers' routes. Hypothermia gets laser-like attention. I watch him order one swimmer pulled out of the 68-degree water during a particularly difficult race and then ask how he recognized the problem. Berger enumerates the classic symptoms: "His lips were purple, his skin was pale, his stroke rate was down, and he didn't know where he was." The swimmer was treated immediately and recovered.

Understanding water and its potential for destruction has only been a priority in the last century and a half. Drowning was a horrific public health issue in the early days of travel by sea. From 1855 to 1875, shipwrecks took the lives of more than 33,000 souls off the coast of England. In the United States some 9,000 people a year were drowning. During one hot July week in 1875, there were 14 deaths by drowning—in a single city, New York. Newspaper editorials called for better supervision and public lessons. "Until the art of swimming becomes more generally practiced," wrote the *New York Times*, "deaths by drowning will be numerous. We do not think it is any exaggeration to say that the majority of the people cannot swim." Ralph Thomas, the aquaphile bibliographer for whom swimming was right up there with breathing, praised the suggestion by Australian Charles Steedman that coroners' verdicts of drowning victims should be changed to "death caused by a most important feature in the physical education of the victim having been com-

pletely ignored, namely, 'the art of swimming.' Perhaps a better one is that there should be a law 'compelling all persons saved from drowning, who were unable to swim, to pay a tithe' of their property to their rescuers."

Two particularly dreadful shipwrecks finally motivated public officials. In 1878, the SS *Princess Alice*, a paddle-steamer running excursion tours on London's Thames, was rammed by a coal ship and split in half. More than 650 people died, many poisoned by the foul sewage in the river. Of the 339 women aboard, only 1 survived. In 1904, a fire from the forward section ignited the wooden decks of the *General Slocum*, a passenger steamboat, sending it to the bottom of New York's East River. It was—until September 11, 2001—the deadliest disaster in the city's history: 1,021 people died, including hundreds of women whose voluminous skirts and petticoats prevented them from swimming to the nearby shore.

Together, those accidents (murders, some called them) led to a number of reforms, including shipboard regulations for passenger safety and increased agreement that women should learn to swim and be allowed to trim their swimming costumes to water-friendly proportions. There was also, for the first time, public agreement on the need for proper life-saving techniques.

"The hardest part of a rescue is keeping them afloat," John Ryan Sr. explains. "So our golden rule on the beach is, if you see somebody in trouble, and there's no lifeguard around, call 911, and get them a flotation device. We can be there in five minutes." Ryan is telling me about the Junior Lifeguard Program in East Hampton, New York, a summer set of classes and drills for youngsters that reflects more than one hundred years of leadership by the American Red Cross and other organizations dedicated to water safety. Today there are programs like it on beaches across the United States, teaching the skills to make ocean swimming efficient and secure. More than 250 youngsters from nine to fourteen are enrolled in this session, both local residents and renters (city folk, Ryan calls them). It fills, Ryan says, a critical need. "I believe that between 40 and 50 percent of the school-age population cannot swim—that they cannot tread water for five minutes at the deep end of the pool. Yet they will go into the ocean with a boogie board. And that's dangerous."

It is a shocking number made more astounding when you consider the geography. The town of East Hampton, a resort and residential community on the very eastern end of New York's Long Island, occupies a chunk of land and beach that narrows to just half a mile at high tide. Parts of it are tony indeed; others, not so much. All of it is surrounded on three sides by water—the Atlantic Ocean, the bays that lead to Long Island Sound, and the sound that straddles both. It's just a finger of land in the sea, a sea that has claimed its share of lives over the years. Not knowing how to swim here is like

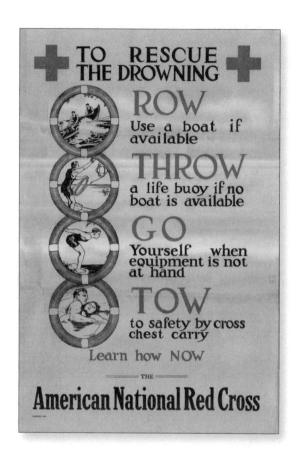

not knowing how to drive at the Indy 500. So Ryan, a white-haired former lifeguard who founded the program twenty years ago, tests the kids during the winter and helps train them in the summer. Not all will graduate to the big chair on the beach as professionals (as Ryan's own nine children all have), but this "makes them safer in the ocean," he says. Which is why he shows up every weekend at the beach, where the kids are taught the right way to respect and enjoy the ocean.

On the Sunday morning I stop by, the four-foot waves are as daunting to me as they are to a pair of eleven-year-old girls, hanging back when directed to swim a drill with the rest of their group. "It's up to you," Robby Lambert, the twenty-nine-year-old coach is saying. "Do you want to work on that really bad four-letter word, F-E-A-R?" The girls aren't sure. Lambert challenges them, lets them decide. "I can't drag a kid into the water," he tells me. "It has to be on their own terms." I point out that the ocean is, um, a bit scary. "It's the same as yesterday, and they went in then," he replies. "I think we just pushed them so much, so last night they were able to build on that fear of, 'Oh, I don't want to go back today.'" Lambert, a surfer by choice and the owner of a plumbing company by profession, gets a small paycheck for teaching. But that's not why he does it. "When you swim, you're taking away one of your senses, your hearing," he says. "So it leaves you the peace of your mind, the cadence of your swim. I love swimming."

I lose sight of the reticent junior lifeguards that morning, but I see Robby and his colleagues surrounded by youngsters at the other activities run by this thoroughly public-spirited group. One foggy afternoon in July they're cheering on the grown-up lifeguards at a multi-town tournament that pits the hunkiest guys and the best-toned gals in the county against each other in everything from run-swim-run races to mock rescues from the rough surf. At the beach the next day, I chat with two of the regulars as they put down their binoculars and trade shifts with their buddies. Like Lambert, most are surfers, square-jawed with rippling muscles, in jammers and back-wards baseball caps, totally dedicated to the people they're there to protect, often picking them up before danger has a chance. The day before, they'd rescued a nine-year-old from a rip tide and a woman in her fifties. "She just brought us cookies," Matt Burns tells me, de-lighted. How did he know to rescue them? "You can see it coming, on their facial expressions. The kid looked panicked." He brought them both in with a cross-chest carry. Matt and his twin, Ryan, are college students, fixtures on this beach in the summer. A third lifeguard, Lee Bertrand, drives up in an ATV to check on the situation. Like all of them, he appreciates the benefits of a summer job on the beach. "It's a pretty good deal if this is your office," he tells me. "Because this is the place you want to come to when you're off."

Lucky for us, they're not off much. At my first open-water swim, a charity event for cancer called Swim Across America, I'm doing half a mile in a choppy bay in Amagansett, the next-door village. At one point I look up and realize we are surrounded by lifeguards, balanced on paddleboards or surf boards, marking the course (and watching us). "There are as many of you as there are of us," I remark to one hunky protector. "That's the way it should be," he says. "Concierge service." I put my head back in the water and stroke on, protected.

Another swimming myth: rolling a drowning victim over a barrel is likely to do more harm than good.

Mer-Mayor

Next time you fly through New York's JFK airport and find yourself gridlocked on the Van Wyck Expressway trying to get to or from the city, consider the man for whom this annoying road was named. You'd rather be swimming? You definitely want Robert A. Van Wyck by your side.

While sitting on the veranda of a Long Island inn one August afternoon in 1898, Van Wyck, then mayor of New York, heard the screams of three young women floundering in nearby Jamaica Bay. Mayor Van Wyck threw off the hat and coat of his "natty lounging clothes," vaulted over a railing, and leaped into the water to rescue the drowning damsels. All were unconscious. He swam them to shore, draped each over a barrel—the preferred mode of artificial respiration back then—and supervised their resuscitation. The ladies survived; the mayor was celebrated; he said anyone would have done the same.

It was his finest hour. The thirty-nine-year-old Democrat, a favorite of "Boss" Tweed's corrupt Tammany Hall, disliked public speaking, and his inauguration speech before 3,000 spectators consisted entirely of the following two sentences: "The people have chosen me to be mayor. I shall say whatever I have to say to them." He should have stuck to swimming: he was not reelected.

9

The Art of
Swimming

alfway across, I start to sing—not aloud, not to freak out the fish or spook another swimmer or leak water into my lungs—just to myself, a jolt from the jukebox playing in my head. The music syncs my stroke; the words press me forward:

> You gotta swim
> And swim when it hurts
> The whole world is watching
> You haven't come this far
> To fall off the earth.

The song is called "Swim."

> Yeah you've gotta swim
> Don't let yourself sink
> Just find the horizon
> I promise you it's not as far as you think.

I'm so drawn to the message, so haunted by the melody, I've adopted it as my anthem for this journey. And the back story is every bit as heroic as what happened here in the Hellespont. Andrew McMahon, the talented young composer/pianist who fronts the band Jack's Mannequin, wrote it after a terrifying year and a half undergoing treatment for leukemia. He'd been diagnosed at age twenty-two, while he was on tour. "My doctor said it was a fifty-fifty shot," Andrew tells me. It was "a brutal experience, with some pretty dark moments." When he came out the other side he was physically healed but emotionally despairing, his self-confidence drained. One night he came across the word "swim" and scrawled it on a piece of paper on his bedside table. The next day he sat down and wrote—"very fast, a one-sitting song," he recalls. "The word 'swim' is so powerful, and it just sort of unfolded itself: 'You've got to swim; you've got to swim.'" The song was an instant hit, with references to greedy politicians and lost love broadening the appeal during turbulent times. "There was an air of things ready to fall apart," Andrew says. "I felt it wasn't just me that was struggling. It wasn't just a song about myself; I tried to connect it back to the people around me. Maybe I wanted to feel that I wasn't alone."

"Swim" broke Andrew's writer's block and became a fixture at every concert, where thousands have come up afterwards to show him the lyrics—his lyrics—tattooed on their ankles and shoulders and chests. SWIM FOR THE MUSIC. JUST KEEP YOUR HEAD ABOVE. SWIM. Right there in black ink. I see a few myself at a twilight performance in New York's Central Park, as the mostly twenty-something audience sings along with him, their sunglasses propped on their heads, their voices rising and falling with the rolling waves of the melody. "It's the most inspirational song I know," says Jennie, twenty-five, who has cerebral palsy and uses a wheelchair. "I always sing it when I'm having a bad day." I ask if she swims. "Yes," she says, beaming. "I can walk in the shallow end of the pool."

Andrew also loves to swim, especially in the surf of Southern California that is now his home. "Being inside of a massive body of water hammers home how infinitely unimportant each of us [is] as individuals, and how much more important each of us [is] in connection to the whole," he says. That connection is what drives him. At a healthy twenty-nine now, a sunny, spirited blond with a radiant grin, who looks as if he were born in blue jeans, he is delighted with the reaction to "Swim." "It's become a letter to people in hard times," he muses. *"I didn't want to write this and have it be a cancer song. I wanted it to be a human song. About struggle in general and finding the hope inside. Luckily, I feel like that's what my fans have taken from it."*

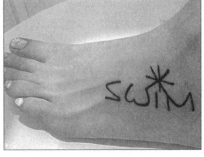

I am also a veteran of the cancer wars, and I know something about struggle. "Swim" is definitely a human song. Which is why it is carrying me across the Hellespont.

In the hands of an artist, the world of swimming, already magical, becomes monumental. Pools transcend gunnite under the brush of David Hockney. The rhythms of the Rhine shimmer in Wagner's "Prelude" to *Das Rheingold*, a series of undulating notes that paint the flow so distinctly, a blind person could see the water. And smart coaches, of both swimming and life, would gladly trade their clipboards for the go-get-'em poetry of Walt Whitman:

> Long have you timidly waded holding a plank by the shore,
> Now I will you to be a bold swimmer,
> To jump off in the midst of the sea, rise again, nod to me, shout,
> and laughingly dash with your hair.

This from a man who teased that his forte was floating. "I was a first-rate aquatic loafer," Whitman, a strong swimmer, once remarked.

Swimming is a perfect setting for romance, especially when it's tragic. Even tragicomic. In Christopher Marlowe's lusty Elizabethan fantasy of Hero and Leander, when the naked Leander emerged from his solo swim (his cloak, you'll recall, still firmly tied to his head), the virgin Hero "screeched for fear. . . . And ran into the dark," a scenario worthy of Jerry Seinfeld, although there is no known Renaissance equivalent of "shrinkage." Marlowe explains Hero's girlish panic with patronizing care: "Such sights as this to tender maids are rare." Two centuries later, Lord Byron included Leander in his self-referential "Don Juan" while describing the Don's own aquatic abilities:

> A better swimmer you could scarce see ever,
> He could, perhaps, have pass'd the Hellespont,
> As once (a feat on which ourselves we prided)
> Leander, Mr. Ekenhead, and I did.

The story has long captured readers' imaginations, including that of a young British pauper named Samuel Taylor Coleridge. Sometime around 1886, while walking down London's Strand, he windmilled his arms as if swimming and accidentally came in contact with a gentleman's waistcoat. When the man seized the lad and accused him of trying to pick his pocket, the terrified youngster explained that he'd been daydreaming, imagining himself Leander swimming across the Hellespont. The gentleman was so taken with his intelligence, he paid his entrance fees to the library, allowing Coleridge "to indulge his love of reading," according to his biographer. It was his ticket to education, and Coleridge ultimately helped create the Romantic Movement. Thus was created the world's first swimming scholarship, enabled by the artful tale of Hero and Leander.

They have also inspired a sequence of oil paintings by Cy Twombly, who used "waves of brushstrokes," according to the Tate Modern, "which cascade across the canvasses." Symphonies and ballads have mourned them through the ages, and a modern artist, Adam Guettel, sings an emotional "Hero and Leander" that soars and sighs with the spray.

Sea Notes

When England's King George III took to the sea at Weymouth, a flock of fiddlers concealed in a nearby bathing machine struck up "God Save the King" to invigorate his royal plunge. Such are the privileges of majesty. Gertrude Ederle crossed the Channel to the amplified sounds of "Let Me Call You Sweetheart," spun from a wax disc on a portable phonograph in the trailing tugboat. She sometimes hummed along. The rest of us rock only to the orchestras in our heads. While waterproof music boxes definitely ease the boredom of long-distance pool laps, serious training, like swimming in open water, demands all the senses. So most swimmers sing from memory, an eclectic catalogue of songs to quicken the limbs and focus the brain.

Lynne Cox has maneuvered through water that's icy enough to chill our drinks. She sings, "One hundred bottles of beer on the wall" by counting up to 1,000 bottles, then back down again, another 1,000 times. She's sung a lot of beer.

Mabel Tidings, Channel-swimming protagonist of Tina Howe's play *Pride's Crossing*, sings "Nursery rhymes mostly. 'Row, Row, Row Your Boat.' 'The Farmer in the Dell.' I sing each one two hundred times and then move on to another." When a friend says she'd go mad, Mabel responds, "It's relaxing, actually."

Diana Nyad sings the *Beverly Hillbillies* theme song. Endlessly. "It's two stanzas, and it keeps me occupied," she tells me. "You need a beat. Not 'Imagine' or k.d. lang singing 'Hallelujah!' You can't swim to that. I'll do Neil Young's 'The Damage Done'—not the whole song, just the chorus. If I sing those two verses 2,000 times, that would be exactly four hours, forty-five minutes. Same with the *Beverly Hillbillies*. The Neil Young is better at night, 'cause it's quiet and has that falsetto voice."

Alan Morrison, who is training for the Channel, sings ten songs, one for each lap (or the laps in his head), from "One" by U2 (Lap 1) to "So Happy Together" by The Turtles (Lap 2), all the way to "Et Misericordia" from Vivaldi's *Magnificat*, no doubt a reflection on the condition of his body by the thousandth or so multiple of Lap 10.

Michael Phelps sings "the last song I heard when I got out of my car. Anything to keep from thinking about looking at the black line for countless hours every day."

The combination of sex and the sea has always been irresistible to songwriters, and nowhere does it resonate more merrily than in popular music that accompanied Americans' giddy discovery of the seashore at the turn of the twentieth century. From the 1890s through the 1920s, song after song turned moon-June-spoon into beach-peach-teach, a simple formula that required only a sunny day, a handsome lifeguard, and a pretty girl who wanted to learn how to swim. "Paul, Won't You Teach Me the Crawl" sings one "little

lass, with plenty of class," her suit "just a trifle too small." By the end of the second verse they get married, and "the baby's now learning to crawl." Art speeds up everything.

Every now and then the tables turn, and it's the girl, not the guy, who can swim. When Jimmy O'Donnell takes Nelly O'Connell down to the beach one day, it's Nell who "took to the water just like Neptune's daughter / Jim couldn't swim a stroke." As you might imagine, the swimmer Nell takes up with is someone Jim "wanted to choke." Nell, however, has room in her heart. She urges, "Hurry up, Jim," and the chorus of "Splash! Splash! Splash!" suggests that he has a chance. Another seriously radical woman is Betsy, "the belle of the bathers / Swimming's considered her forte." The women are jealous, especially the fat ones (I am quoting here), "For all of them men shun / and pay no attention / whenever fair Betsy is near." Not surprisingly, no one lives happily ever after in this song.

In this tittering milieu of double entendres and daring courtship, the rhymes give the clues: The occupant of a bathing suit is usually a beaut. And what she needs to know about water is that no one oughter tell her mother what's going on. Mothers are key in beach

parlor music. "Don't Go in the Water, Daughter," urges one song— "A girl's a sight / And looks a fright / The moment she gets wet." No chance for romance there. "Don't Take Your Beau to the Seashore," commands another (this one by Irving Berlin), rhyming the role of a petticoat (to "conceal") with the reality of a bathing suit (to "reveal"), bad news for imperfect bodies. Uh-oh. Reality is never more brutal than in "The Handsome, Brave Life Saver," in which Miss Liza, who "rav'd about the wave / And every Sunday went to bathe" never doubted that if she swam too far the (yes) "handsome, brave life saver" would bring her in. Except that one day she "strayed" beyond where she could "wade / She "grew afraid," called him "to her aid," in fact "cried for help three times or more. / But he was busy on the shore." Turns out "his wife was standing near / That's why he couldn't hear." Sometimes life sucks, even at the beach.

My favorite sheet music of the time is less callous, more suggestive, and far more generous to the sensibilities of both the big guy and the cute ("in her bathing suit") gal. The loving couple would meet every summer at the beach and—well, let's let the lyricist tell it:

And she'd say to him, Come on let's go in
So he'd take her by the hand.
Then they'd . . .

CHORUS:

Swim for a while, out in the ocean
Then down they would go—way down below
Nobody knew what they went down there to do
But they'd come up laughing in a minute or two
Then they'd swim for a while, out in the ocean
And down to the bottom once more
When the water got rough,
She'd holler, John, that's enough
Then they had to swim back to the shore.

Ev'ry single minute of the day
They're either swimming or loving away
They ride the donkeys, chute the chutes
They don't care what happens to their bathing suits . . .

You get the idea. Even swimming has its *scandales*.

In 1935 a more urbane composer produced an even more delectable song. Cole Porter, a suave regular at society's finest pools and lidos, collaborated with Moss Hart on the musical comedy *Jubilee*, a witty (although now dated) spoof on an unnamed royal family that could only reside at Buckingham Palace. Bored with their regal lives, each goes off to satisfy a private fantasy in the common world. The queen's dream is swimming. She arranges to meet "the naked swimmer who went into the films"—an actor nicknamed Mowgli who is a biting caricature of the Olympian-turned-Tarzan, Johnny Weissmuller. By the end of Act I the queen is in the pool with Mowgli and his mermen, jubilantly proclaiming the value of her newfound activity:

> There's nothing like swimming for trimming the old physique,
> For giving the torso that certain chic;
> There's nothing that hustles the muscles and makes 'em tauter
> Than gaily doing your daily dozen with Neptune's daughter.

The peppy melody and brilliant rhymes (Porter couples the queen's "regalia" with the crawl from "Australia") are beyond charming; unfortunately, almost no one knows the song. It was dropped from the show before it opened on Broadway, and when *Jubilee* closed after only 169 performances, it was consigned to the archives. Today a number of revivals have restored this lost gem to their productions, but "There's Nothing Like Swimming" has yet to find a slot on iTunes.

Literature has always taken swimming more seriously, with a flood of established metaphors: the loneliness of the ocean, the flux of the current, the peace or finality of the deep. The sea is the womb, or our unconscious, or both. Pools make us happy, or vulnerable, or anxious. Swimming represents the possible and the impossible. It's an obsession that cracks the glass surface of life, a river that gets you to places you only imagined. Learning to swim is a parable of survival; marathons conquer the challenge of distance. Water is holy, and swimming is a kind of communion, as Camus suggests in *The Plague*. Water makes you weird, as Alice learned in Wonderland. Water demands risk, as F. Scott Fitzgerald wrote, turning the imagery onto his own craft: "All good writing is swimming under water and holding your breath." Roger Deakin, whose book *Waterlog* chronicles his year swimming the wild water of Britain, described diving in. "You let yourself go, launch out, cross over some sort of boundary. Looking out at a black sheet of water is like contemplating a blank sheet of paper—but once you are in, you are in."

Writers who swim know the secret handshake. "Swimming is the apex of the day, its heart," wrote John Cheever, whose 1964 short story, "The Swimmer," makes the activity he loved the core of a searing allegory. It begins as a perfect summer Sunday for Neddy Merrill, a Connecticut exurbanite with an athlete's body and a millionaire's estate. "The day was beautiful," Cheever writes, "and it seemed to him that a long swim might enlarge and celebrate its beauty." Neddy's course is unique: a "string of swimming pools, that quasi-subterranean stream that curved across the county. . . . He would name the stream Lucinda after his wife." It is an enticing plan—to swim home via his neighbors' pools, a sapphire trail that only a real-life swimmer might have invented. But the Lucinda River weaves instead through raucous cocktail parties, old lovers, and older memories, a surreal journey taking Neddy through spiritual desolation to the abandoned wreck of his house. The last word of the story is "empty," which perfectly describes Neddy's life, clarified finally through the act of swimming.

"My father loved pools," the writer Susan Cheever tells me over dinner one night. "But he wouldn't build one. He liked swimming in other peoples' pools. He swam a very choppy crawl, never learned to breathe right." She uses the same word—"choppy"—that John Cheever uses to describe Neddy's stroke. And she goes on to decode the brilliance of the work. "It was a novel first," she says. "But he burned it." I am dumbfounded. Burned his own novel? How come? "Creative genius," Susan explains definitively. "Then he turned it into a short story. That's why it's so good. By winnowing it down he gave it tremendous power."

The director Frank Perry turned "The Swimmer" into an equally searing film (completed by director Sidney Pollack), for which actor Burt Lancaster had to learn to swim, an ironic indication of how far swimming had fallen out of favor by 1968. Hollywood's earliest swimming stars weren't just curvy actors who could swim; they were authentic aquanauts whose movies were often about swimming itself. Annette Kellerman reinterpreted her vaudeville act for California's new industry and made a dozen silent movies from 1909 to 1924—*Neptune's Daughter, Venus of the South Seas, Daughter of the Gods*, to name a few. By today's standards, most were sappy underwater fantasies, heavy on fairytale and exotic—sometimes outlandish—mermaid costumes. It was even a tough sell then. "What! A woman fish on the screen!" yelped one studio head, almost refusing the pitch. But the movies made money, lots of money, and Kellerman's fabulous physique and gutsy maneuvers (she swam all her own stunts), along with a shoal of personally trained mer-chorus girls, kept the audiences buying tickets. Sometimes she forgot the fishtail, and the rest of the garb as well, a tribute to her perfect body that the studio was delighted to promote. "You won't strain your eyes trying to follow the flitting forms of these darting divinities of the deep," promised one industry magazine. "You get more than a flash—much more. This is the naked truth." In 1917, she was cited as an example when censors banned nudity in future films.

In Kellerman's wake came a quartet of elite athletes who slid directly from the pool to show business. Eleanor Holm won gold in the backstroke at the 1932 Olympics but was banned from the next games because she drank champagne aboard the ship taking her to Germany, a moment of Olympic prudery that made her turn professional. Her only movie was *Tarzan's Revenge* (1938), in which she executes a snappy backstroke and an Olympian crawl to escape from a crocodile in the jungle river. "They had wired the jaws shut, so I wasn't bitten by it," she told a reporter, "but it could swipe you with that big tail. I was scared to death!" The rest of Holm's career centered on giant public stages, most notably as one of the headliners of the famed Aquacade produced by her second husband, Billy Rose, at the 1939 World's Fair. Her costar there was another Olympian, the magnificently muscular Johnny Weissmuller.

Born in Romania, raised mainly in Chicago, Weissmuller won five golds and one bronze in two Olympics (1924, 1928) and set sixty-seven world records, with such a wicked crawl that a coach once told him he "fairly climbed out of the water." When Weissmuller retired at twenty-five, he had never lost a race. He was handsome, too. And he became the definitive (but not the first) Tarzan, swinging through twelve movies to the accompaniment of his signature yodel-yell. Also swimming like a champ—with his head out of the water (the better for the camera to catch him) in *Tarzan and the Ape Man* (1932) and in the famously sexy underwater romp in the follow-up, *Tarzan and His Mate*. That's the swim scene you really want to see—although it's not clear whether costar Maureen O'Sullivan or her double, Olympian Josephine McKim, is the nude swimmer. Yes, nude. 1934. So much for the censors. Weissmuller, however, keeps his loincloth on.

The other famous swimming Tarzan was Buster Crabbe, who became even better known for his roles as Flash Gordon and Buck

Johnny Weissmuller:
brilliant swimmer,
charming Tarzan

Rogers. He was a formidable real-life action figure at two Olympics,
1928 (bronze) and 1932 (gold), after which he too swam in the Aquacade, opposite Eleanor Holm.

There was one more Aquacade megastar, one more of these early
crossover sports figures, a genuine celebrity who could bring folks
to the edge of the water and drop their jaws, could open a movie
and keep the audience asking for more. For many of us in the 1950s,
there was only one movie mermaid, only one Hollywood photo on
our walls. Every girl I grew up with wanted to be Esther Williams.
Actually, I wanted to be June Allyson first but then decided that
waterproof hair and a sexy stroke were way more interesting than
a smoky voice.

You could run out of fingers counting the reasons Esther Williams
remains a hero: her teenage records in freestyle and breaststroke,

her smashing performances in the San Francisco Aquacade with Weissmuller, a body that was built to fill a bathing suit, and a smile that tested every shade of Technicolor. Her smooth strokes and elegant dives looked so effortless, you believed you could do them too. But the reason I most adore Esther Williams is because she played the game and beat them at it. As she tells the story in her hilarious autobiography, *The Million Dollar Mermaid*, she wasn't looking for a career in show biz—she wanted only to swim and to win. Her first screen test, at 20th Century Fox, confirmed it. The casting director told her, "You're a swimmer, right? Well, get back into the pool." And so she did. When World War II cancelled America's participation in the 1940 Olympics, Williams turned pro but figured the Aquacade was all the show biz she could handle. MGM had another idea. The popularity of a new movie sensation at 20th Century Fox—ice skater Sonja Henie and a series of films in which she glided across the frost to music—sparked the copycat instinct at MGM. They tried Williams again because the head of the studio, Louis B. Mayer, had issued a dictum: "Melt the ice, get a swimmer, make it pretty!" And that's how Esther Williams became our hero—because Hollywood needed a new gimmick to outsell a proven gimmick and because she did it with style and skill and, always, that smile.

Despite "being pushed around by little guys with big libidos," Williams (five foot eight, often wearing three-inch heels) helped invent a new Hollywood genre: the swimming extravaganza, a musical comedy with an elaborate, multi-mermaid swimathon, choreographed by Busby Berkeley to showcase her talents and to be geometrically stunning from every single angle. Picking up where Annette Kellerman had left off, Esther Williams also turned synchronized swimming into a popular art form, ultimately helping to make it an official Olympic sport. She swam on-screen with everyone from Mickey Rooney (*Andy Hardy's Double Life*) to cat-and-mouse team Tom and Jerry (*Dangerous When Wet*). She made the frothy es-

Esther Williams as Annette Kellerman in *Million Dollar Mermaid*

capism of *Neptune's Daughter* and *Bathing Beauty* as mouthwatering as popcorn. And she was the natural choice to play the lead in Kellerman's life story, *Million Dollar Mermaid*, in 1952. What she later told an interviewer about her predecessor defines her own life as well. "She knew there was more to being a woman than being kept in corsets," Williams said of Kellerman. "She wasn't content to float. She was determined to swim. What she did was to persuade women to get in the water. I'm a continuum of that."

In 1993, when Asphalt Green, a gigantic new swimming facility, opened in Manhattan, the ceremony included a tribute to Esther Williams. Jane Katz performed the synchro to honor the star and spoke with her just before the show. Williams's advice is her legacy. "Swim pretty!" she said. That's life imitating art.

Wetflix

First, every Esther Williams movie. Then,
every Tarzan. Next:

Sunset Boulevard (1950)—"The poor dope!
He always wanted a pool. Well, in the end,
he got himself a pool—only the price turned
out to be a little high."

The Graduate (1967)— "Just one word." "Yes, sir."
"Plastics." Two more: swimming pool.

The Swimmer (1968)—The iconic swimming movie.
Joan Rivers has a cameo.

The Swimming Pool (*La Piscine*) (1969)—A gorgeous
pool. And a murder.

The Abyss (1989)—Voluntary hypothermia saves the
heroine. It's possible.

Est-Ouest (1999)—Cold war, cold-water escape from postwar
Soviet Union. "Keep swimming," he's told. "It's your only
chance."

Watermarks (2004)—Even Hitler couldn't extinguish the swimming spirit.

On a Clear Day (2005)— "How mad would you have to be to
swim this?" "Totally."

Swimming Upstream (2005)— "In Australia where I grew up,
summers were long and hot. Water changed that. It
kept you alive and safe. At least for a . . . while."

Pride (2007)— "Brothers don't swim. Until the
coach gets hold of them."

Men Who Swim (2010)—Swedish all-male
synchro team finds the meaning of
midlife in the swimming pool.

10

Swim

SUDDENLY, I'M CLOSE. *The marker boat has moved, unannounced; the red balloons deflated. So much for trust. But as I turn south, the currents shift as predicted. I can't say I've found my enGENE, but I'm definitely on the home stretch. "Stay left! Stay left!" warns Fiona, my friendly, peripatetic coach, yelling through a megaphone as her boat steers me from the swifter current that might take me . . . somewhere else. I've been swimming more than an hour, and the deadline is closing in, but so is the finish line. I can see the ramp, the pier, the walls of the ancient castle lining the shore. Just keep swimming, I tell myself, channeling Dory; "SWIM," Andrew sings, and I listen. The last hundred yards are fierce. I'm fighting a strong current that makes the trees on the shore stand still. I pull hard from a safe deposit box of strength I didn't know I had left, my reserves kicking in.*

"You made it, Lynn! You made it!" shouts Fiona, cheering me into the dock.

And then I do. Quietly, finally, I'm there. Confirmation comes seconds later, when I leap out of the water—("It's not how you swim; it's how you finish," another swimmer has told me)—and cross the red carpet, not a celebrity photo corral but a computerized timer that reads the chip around my ankle to certify my time. *Ding! I did it!* Waded into the water in Europe and walked out in Asia. Crossed the Hellespont in time and emerged on earth on my own two feet. I flip off my goggles, shake out my wet hair, take the towel I am handed, and join my competitors, who are milling around and celebrating their own swims. A friend grabs my arm.

"Lynn, look up!"

The leader board, a giant electronic scorecard flashing the results for every category, reads

1. Lynn Sherr. USA 1:24:16.

I have, improbably, won my age group. I start to smile, then catch myself being competitive. Will it hold? I burst into laughter. Of course it will. I am, it turns out, the only woman in my age group. There are more ancient categories, but I've got mine covered.

I wish I could tell you that I humbly accepted my accomplishment and moved on to other things. That as the sun slid from Asia to Europe, I turned into a grown-up and left my swim behind me. No way. I grin like a schoolgirl as we high-five each other and mentally reswim the course ("Did you feel the enGENE?" "Which route did you take?" "Did you ever see the red balloons?"), and when I mount the little podium during the late afternoon award ceremony, I am every inch an Olympian. Arms up, victory smile. Duck my head graciously for the ribbon with the medal. A medal! Byron only caught a cold for his efforts. I wear it to the celebratory dinner that night, a grand joke approved by the very generous crowd. The next day at breakfast, I finally put it aside. "Morning, champ," says a British firefighter who outswam me by half an hour. "Where's the medal?" He, like all my new pals—all of whom finished the race—agrees that I don't have to explain to anyone back home that my medal was not completely competitive.

Look, I know that four-hundred-some people swam faster than I did. And that even at age fourteen I couldn't have kept up with the Turkish teen who won the whole thing in forty-two slippery minutes, half my time. And I know that Leander swam it both ways, at night, straight across the current. But as Byron told a friend about his own one-way journey, "Nothing is impossible in love or religion. If I had had a Hero on the other side, perhaps I should have worked harder." Me too. In fact, I swam four miles, a personal record. I beat more than a few people. The training, the tips, the hard work all paid off. As my official T-shirt says, "Leander, Lord Byron . . . and ME!" Try prying that off my back.

Months after the event, I still turn to the map, my eyes darting straight to the strait as I say to myself, over and over, "I started there and ended there, swam from Europe to Asia. I swam the Hellespont." I can still feel the glow. Still feel the pride. Still feel embraced by the blend of turquoise Aegean with deep Black Sea, buoying me as I glided across. We did it together, the water and I. It held me up; I pushed myself through. We were partners—always are—because you can't do it alone. This, then, is why I swim.

Success!

"It's the best swim I ever had," agrees Clare Rooke, a robust forty-four-year-old physics professor from London who convinced her two younger brothers to join her (creating the only brother-sister combo in the Hellespont) and came in fourth in her age group at a breakneck fifty-four minutes. Even taking time to smell the roses. "I knew it was a race, but I stopped in the middle, took off my goggles, and said to myself, 'There's Europe, there's Asia, and here's me. And I'm in the middle of it.'" Clare swims for peace of mind. "It cocoons me," she says. "No sound, no one can find me. It's a mind game." Several weeks later she emails to announce that she's rejoined a local swim club to train every week. "Swimming for me has always been more than keeping fit," she writes. "I love the sense of freedom in the open water and the calmness of the rhythm of my strokes and breathing. The feeling of full submersion is just wonderful and a perfect tonic to the stresses of a busy life."

Lisa Crawford, who signed up for the swim just hoping to finish and wound up around the middle of the pack, is ecstatic. The race was her way to forget turning forty. "Yuck. I decided I needed a personal challenge to mark this less than groovy milestone," she tells me beforehand. Swimming "is the simplicity of following that little blue line—boring for some, but I have a son with autism who is quite challenging. So it's a great way to switch off and not be bothered by anything or anyone. Training for this race has been great, to do something just for me." Lisa, a stay-at-home mom, used to be a solicitor in London. "Swimming in the sea felt really serene," she says. "I expect that was a lot to do with the calm seas and sunshine but also in swimming in the same direction as all the other swimmers, who were there to try to achieve their goal. We were alone but also together for an hour or so, which was a lovely feeling. And although it was a race, it didn't feel that way to me. I even stopped to talk to one or two people in the middle of the strait mainly to try to ascertain the whereabouts of the promised red balloon, and that was quite amusing and slightly surreal!"

Everyone exults. Joe Nassar from Jackson, Mississippi, is grinning broadly, still wearing his cap and goggles ten minutes after crossing the line because "I'm a little too sore to take them off!" He swam with his business partner because "the wind and the water kicked my tail last year and I didn't finish. This time, it was great." A father and son from Edinburgh finish together: "I'll do it if you'll do it," they'd agreed. David Morris, from Alexandria, Virginia, drawls, "I'd roll over and look at the mountain and think, 'Good Gertie, I'm not even halfway across!' And then I looked over, and I thought, 'Oh my goodness, it's there!' And instead of trying to beat my time, I just enjoyed the moment. I just swam the Hellespont, doggone!" Joel Stratte-McClure, an adventurer from San Francisco who is trekking the Mediterranean, called his bronze medal "a walk in the park. I think I compensated too much—went too far to Istanbul [north] before I cut over to Greece [south]. But what the hell, I mean it's a 5,000-mile journey; a couple of kilometers here and there don't matter." Kate Bischof, the fish from Perth, streaked across in 47:07, the second non-Turkish woman over the line, first in her age group. "I couldn't figure out where to turn," she confesses. "It wasn't what they showed us. No whooshing current to take me down there." Never felt the enGENE. "But there must have been something helping me, even if I couldn't detect it. I'd never have done it under an hour." Another Aussie, Irene Keel, has come from Brisbane, where she runs her own accounting and auditing firm. At seventy, a gray-haired dynamo, she has won her age group; like me, she was the only woman in it. She laughingly acknowledges the benefits of growing older and tells me that she took up swimming when she was fifty because of a bad back. "When I started I couldn't swim fifty meters," she says. Now she's winning races around the world. Is swimming an escape, I ask? "Yes, it's a way to chill out for a while," she says, beaming. "All you do is concentrate on your swimming or you drown!"

The next day, the sea looks even more glorious—a deep, rich Mediterranean blue that underscores our accomplishment like a giant magic marker. "It's geography," Bernie Stone, the continent bridger, has told me. "It's tangible. These are the geographical splits of the world. We all know it used to be one. We're just swimming across the folds."

And across history. I've paid tribute to Leander and his Hero, visited the nearby ruins of Troy, where the windy plains described by Homer still evoke the grand sweep of antiquity. And like all the participants in this international race, I realize that the same activity that has expanded my personal universe has also made the world smaller. As the organizers said at the awards ceremony, "Once upon a time we had battles on this landscape; now we share friendship through swimming."

I started this book as a swimmer with a passion; I end it understanding more about why. Yes, we were once fish, but it's not natural, it's not primordial, we were not born to swim; yes, we become buoyant, but it's not easy, and it's certainly not convenient. We've updated the strokes, and we cheer on our Olympians, but it's not new, and it's not really mainstream. It demands concentration, and you are always counting in the water, but it also allows the suspension of time, the flights of fancy. And the color—the colors—so many variations on the shade of blue. Poet Wallace Stevens called it "the basic slate, the universal hue."

Swimming, unlike most addictions, is actually good for us, perhaps even better than we thought. And the more we swim, the bigger the benefits. A year ago I stretched out lazy laps for thirty minutes at a time, generally in warm weather, in pools, by myself, on autopilot; now I race through an hour or more, at the crack of dawn, indoors when it's cold or in the ocean when it's more agreeable, often with other people. And I focus on my stroke. I'll never be a racer, can't come near the perfection of the elites. Unlike them, I have a land life; I play tennis. But my freestyle is faster and sleeker, my breathing less stressed. My shoulders are broader, and the new muscles sometimes cry out for attention. But it's still the best full-body massage available. Olympian Donna deVarona, now sixty-four, swam immediately after a recent hip operation and still swims several times a week. When I ask how long she'll continue, she shoots back, laughing, "As long as I can keep climbing out of the pool!"

Water heals. "If I go in like a cranky sea lion, I come out like a smiling dolphin," said California endurance swimmer Carol Sing in 1999, after she became the then-oldest woman (at fifty-seven) to swim the English Channel. That was two years after she became the oldest woman to cross California's Catalina Channel. "The image is still valid," she tells me. "I'm still swimming and still loving it. I don't think I'm as cranky as I used to be, but it's still great therapy and makes me happy and mellow." It's the world's cheapest antidepressant, the second-best way I know to fall asleep. Or maybe the first. The French poet Paul Valéry wrote of swimming as his love, the sea as his lover. "In it, I am the man I want to be."

The intimacy was less narcissistic for Gertrude Ederle. "To me the sea is like a person—like a child that I've known a long time," she said thirty years after her Channel swim. "It sounds crazy, I know, but when I swim in the sea I talk to it. I never feel alone when I'm out there."

An Actual Bear

Katmai Peninsula on the southwest coast of Alaska is the salmon-catching capital of the country, for both humans and bears. Two-legged fishermen migrate here every summer for their fill of fish; brown bears wait all year for the two-week period when the salmon are spawning, then position themselves on the perilous waterfalls, and swoop up breakfast, lunch, and dinner for the year to come. It is a glorious site. And yet another example of the glory of the water.

Many years ago, at Katmai on vacation, my husband looked out the window of the communal dining hall and motioned me over. "Look!" he said, pointing at the rocky beach no more than fifty yards away. A bear had come down from the woods and was lumbering toward the shore of Naknek Lake, giving some of us a momentary fright. We needn't have wasted the adrenalin. Paying us no mind, the giant creature walked straight into the water, deftly maneuvering through the waves until he was about twenty yards out. And then, as we watched in awe, he proceeded to body surf like a champ, riding the waves in and swimming back out, ducking into the water and rising to clear his head. At one point he flipped onto his back, looking more like a hairy guy in a bathtub than a killer creature. His dip lasted at least twenty minutes, with all of us visitors watching slack-jawed. Then the bear swam in, shook off, and returned to the forest. He knew something, that fellow, about the joy of swimming.

So what's next after you've swum the Hellespont—or the Channel, or the Island, or your laps, or just from one end to the other? Annette Kellerman, who died in 1975 at eighty-eight, never stopped dreaming. "This love of the unknown is the greatest of all the joys which swimming has for me," she wrote. "Though my swimming has earned me a goodly fortune I am still looking for my chest of gold in a cool dripping sea cave. Though a professional mermaid for the movies I still wait to see my first real one sitting on a damp grey rock combing her long green hair."

Americans today have a more practical wish list. When a recent poll asked which sport they'd like to participate in, every age group listed swimming for fitness either first or second. That's telling: people *want* to swim. And judging by the increase in enrollment at US Masters Swimming, they also want to swim better. You can always get faster, but there will always be someone faster than you. Slower, too. Swimming doesn't have to be about winning. An earlier admirer called Leander's swim "the crack performance of antiquity"; Byron's, his "ultra achievement." I like to think other adventures still await me. Because there's always another ocean, another pool, another wave, another continental divide. And another generation.

Last summer, my four-year-old grandson, Tyler, continued to progress through Swimmees and Floaties and the usual childish flailing at the pool, often watching me as I did my daily laps. I had no idea how closely. Months later, during his evening bath (goggles on, of course), he announced to his mom, "I want to swim like Lynn." And proceeded to flap his arms in nine inches of water. The next day at his regular swim lesson, he flabbergasted the teacher—and my daughter-in-law—by jumping into the pool and executing a brief but perfectly acceptable freestyle, the first of his tiny life. The smile on his face could have melted the Arctic. The one on mine is still there. This, too, is why I swim.

Acknowledgments

This time I begin with Esther Newberg, whose enthusiasm for yet another of my obsessions changed the course of my life for a remarkable year. Thank you. I am also indebted to Alice Hummer, editor of *Wellesley Magazine*, whose early interest in my aquatic adventures sparked the first tiny version of this book. I could go way back, to the patient camp counselors who first got me into the lake in my itchy wool bathing suit and, of course, to untold armies of frogs, who unknowingly eased my way into the water. But how do you thank an amphibian?

I am especially grateful to the following individuals: Sharon Young, who swam every wave of the Hellespont with me without ever having to get wet; my USMS swim buddies at the Vanderbilt YMCA (and our relentless coach Jonathan Dickson), who have allowed me to draft along their speedy pace; my swim pals from Curaçao, who never made fun of the newbie in the slow lane—and especially Boris Talan, who got me there in the first place; Joel Stager and Colleen McCracken and the talented scientists at Indiana University, for opening up the vault; Bruce Wigo, for sharing his passion and knowledge at the International Swimming Hall of Fame; Simon Murie, Fiona Southwell, and the entire SwimTrek team, who made the Hellespont a fabulous and safe adventure; Donna deVarona, forever an Olympian; Lynne Cox, who has opened the seas for everyone; Ellen Goodman and Nola Safro, for early, critical readings.

For their expertise in various aspects of swimming or its background, I also thank Dean Kamen; Dr. Raj Mittal; Neil Schwartz, Sporting Goods Manufacturers Association; Dan Kasen, National Sporting Goods Association; Charles Sprawson; Cullen Jones; Rowdy Gaines; John Ryan Sr.; Dan Johnson; Dick Covert; Lisa Grepps, Association of Pool & Spa Professionals; Sarah Hayes, CDC; Charles Kroll; Rabbi Anne Ebersman; al-Husein N. Madhany; Richard A. Pegg, PhD; John Knott; Dr. Neil Shubin; George Block; Terry Laughlin; Jane Katz; Dick Ebersol; Karen Crouse; Miriam Ruzow; Ernie Burgess; Judy Foreman; David Clark; Carol Sing; Andrew McMahon; Ellie Waite; for Speedo, Audra Silverman, Kate Wilton, and Jim Gerson; Sandra Davidoff; Laurie Kilmartin; Pat Caddell; and Diana Nyad.

Thanks also to Ivonne Schmid, Kirsten Pires, Elaine Krugman, Bob Brier, Jeff McKay, Steven Sander, Mel Miller, Roberta Staats, Cressida Brown, and Debbie Hesse (USA Swimming Foundation). And to the exceptional folks at PublicAffairs: Clive Priddle, Melissa Raymond, Pete Garceau, Pauline Brown.

As usual, my personal armada of friends and family both tolerated and facilitated my preoccupation. Starting tomorrow, the mouse pad that accompanied this work—"EAT SLEEP SWIM WRITE"—goes away. Thank you all for your patience.

Selected Bibliography

Many of the hundreds of books and articles and websites I consulted are mentioned within the text; here are specifics for some of them, and the best of the rest:

Books and Articles

Blossom, Laurel, ed. *Splash! Great Writing About Swimming.* Hopewell, NJ: Ecco Press, 1996.

Brewster, Edwin Tenney. *Swimming.* Boston: Houghton Mifflin, 1910.

Broady, Bill. *Swimmer.* London: Flamingo, 2000.

Busch, Akiko. *Nine Ways to Cross a River: Midstream Reflections on Swimming and Getting There from Here.* New York: Bloomsbury, 2007.

Byron, George Gordon. *Letters and Journals.* London: J. Murray, 1982.

Catlin, George. *Letters and Notes on the Manners, Customs, and Conditions of the North American Indians.* 2 volumes. 1844. Reprint, New York: Dover, 1973.

Colwin, Cecil. *Breakthrough Swimming.* Champaign, IL: Human Kinetics, 2002.

Corsan, George H. *At Home in the Water.* New York: Young Men's Christian Association Press, 1910.

Counsilman, James "Doc." *The Science of Swimming.* Englewood Cliffs, NJ: Prentice-Hall, 1968.

Courtivron, M. le vicomte de. *Traité complet de natation: Essai sur son application à l'art de la guerre.* Paris: Chez à Phian de La Forest, 1835.

Cox, Lynne. *Grayson.* New York: Alfred A. Knopf, 2006.

———. *Swimming to Antarctica: Tales of a Long-Distance Swimmer.* New York: Alfred A. Knopf, 2005.

"Craven." In *Walker's Manly Exercises.* Philadelphia: John W. Moore, 1856.

Dahlberg, Tim, with Mary Ederle Ward and Brenda Greene. *America's Girl: The Incredible Story of How Swimmer Gertrude Ederle Changed the Nation.* New York: St. Martin's Press, 2009.

Dalton, Frank Eugen. *Swimming Scientifically Taught.* New York: Funk & Wagnalls, 1912.

Dawson, Kevin. "Enslaved Swimmers and Divers in the Atlantic World." *Journal of American History* (March 2006): 1327–1355.

Deakin, Roger. *Waterlog: A Swimmer's Journey Through Britain.* London: Vintage Books, 2000.

Dean, Penny. *Open Water Swimming.* Champaign, IL: Human Kinetics, 1998.

Digby, Sir Everard. *De Arte Natandi libri duo . . . .* London: Thomas Dawson, 1587.

Douglas, W. G. *Spalding's Athletic Library: Swimming.* New York: American Sports, 1894.

Elyot, Sir Thomas. *The Boke, Named the Governour.* London: Thomas East, 1580.

Franklin, Benjamin. *The Autobiography of Benjamin Franklin.* New York: J. B. Alden, 1891.

Fraser, Dawn, with Harry Gordon. *Below the Surface.* William Morrow, 1965.

Frost, J. *Scientific Swimming.* London: Darton, Harvey, and Darton, 1816.

Gibson, Emily, with Barbara Firth. *The Original Million Dollar Mermaid: The Annette Kellerman Story.* Crows Nest, NSW: Allen & Unwin, 2005.

Homer. *The Iliad.* Translated by Robert Fagles. New York: Viking, 1990.

———. *The Odyssey.* Translated by Robert Fagles. New York: Viking, 1996.

Jerome, John. *Blue Rooms: Ripples, Rivers, Pools, and Other Waters.* New York: Henry Holt, 1997.

Kellerman, Annette. *How to Swim.* New York: George H. Doran, 1918.

Klein, Kelly. *Pools.* New York: Rizzoli, 2007.

Laughlin, Terry. *Total Immersion: Swimming That Changes Your Life.* New Paltz, NY: Total Immersion Swimming, 2012.

Leahy, John. "Sergeant." In *The Art of Swimming in the Eton Style.* London: Macmillan, 1875.

Middleton, Christofer. *A Short Introduction for to Learne to Swimme.* London: James Roberts for Edward White, 1595.

Mortimer, Gavin. *The Great Swim.* New York: Walker, 2008.

Nelligan, Richard Francis. *The Art of Swimming: A Practical Working Manual.* Boston: American Gymnasium Company, 1906.

Orme, Nicholas. *Early British Swimming, 56 BC–AD 1719: With the First Swimming Treatise in English, 1595.* Exeter: University of Exeter Press, 1983.

Percey, William. *The Compleat Swimmer: or, The Art of Swimming.* London: J. C. for Henry Fletcher, at the Three Cups in Paul's Church-yard, near the West-End, 1658.

Schollander, Don. *Deep Water.* New York: Ballantine Books, 1971.

Shubin, Neil. *Your Inner Fish: A Journey into the 3.5 Billion-Year History of the Human Body.* New York: Pantheon Books, 2008.

Sinclair, Archibald, and William Henry. *Swimming.* London: Longmans, Green, 1916.

Southgate, Martha. *The Taste of Salt: A Novel.* Chapel Hill, NC: Algonquin Books, 2011.

Sprawson, Charles. *Haunts of the Black Masseur: The Swimmer as Hero.* New York: Pantheon Books, 1992.

Stager, Joel M., and David A. Tanner, eds. *Swimming.* 2nd edition. Handbook of Sports Medicine and Science. Malden, MA: Blackwell Science, 2005.

Steedman, Charles. *Manual of Swimming.* Melbourne: H. T. Dwight, 1867.

Stout, Glenn. *Young Woman & the Sea: How Trudy Ederle Conquered the English Channel and Inspired the World.* Boston: Houghton Mifflin Harcourt, 2009.

Swimmer, An Experienced. *The Science of Swimming.* New York: Fowlers and Wells, 1849.

Thévenot, Melchisédich. *The Art of Swimming.* 3rd edition. London: John Lever.

Thomas, Ralph. *Swimming: With Lists of Books Published in English, German, French and Other European Languages, and Critical Remarks on the Theory and Practice of Swimming and Resuscitation.* London: S. Low, Marston, 1904.

Torres, Dara. *Age Is Just a Number: Achieve Your Dreams at Any Stage in Your Life.* New York: Broadway Books, 2009.

van Leeuwen, Thomas A. P. *The Springboard in the Pond: An Intimate History of the Swimming Pool.* Edited by Helen Searing. Cambridge, MA: MIT Press, 1999.

Wagenvoord, James. *The Swim Book.* Indianapolis: Bobbs-Merrill, 1980.

Watson, Kathy. *The Crossing: The Glorious Tragedy of the First Man to Swim the English Channel.* New York: Jeremy P. Archer/Putnam, 2000.

Weissmuller, Johnny. *Swimming the American Crawl.* Boston: Houghton Mifflin, 1930.

Wigo, Bruce. *The Golden Age of Swimming: A Pictorial History of the Sport & Pools That Changed America.* Bruce Wigo, 2009.

Williams, Esther, with Digby Diehl. *The Million Dollar Mermaid.* New York: Simon & Schuster, 1999.

Wilson, William. *The Swimming Instructor.* London: Horace Cox, 1883.

Wiltse, Jeff. *Contested Waters: A Social History of Swimming Pools in America.* Chapel Hill: University of North Carolina Press, 2007.

Poetry

The Hero and Leander myth is recounted in Virgil's *Georgics*, in Ovid's *Heroides*, and most fully in the poem "Hero and Leander" by the Greek poet Musaeus, who lived in the sixth century CE. Christopher Marlowe's version was published in 1598; it was finished by George Chapman when Marlowe died.

Byron, Lord (George Gordon). *Don Juan.* Halifax: Milner and Sowerby, 1837. www.gutenberg.org/files/21700/21700-h/21700-h.htm.

Sexton, Anne. "The Nude Swim." In *Love Poems.* Boston: Houghton Mifflin, 1969.

Stevens, Wallace. "Le monocle de mon oncle." In *Harmonium.* New York: Alfred A. Knopf, 1923.

Surveys, Reports, and Other Sources

The Association of Pool and Spa Professionals. "U.S. Swimming Pool and Hot Tub Market 2011." www.apsp.org/utility/showDocumentFile/?objectID=684.

National Center for Injury Prevention and Control. "Unintentional Drowning: Fact Sheet." Centers for Disease Control and Prevention. www.cdc.gov/homeandrecreationalsafety/water-safety/water injuries-factsheet.html.

National Sporting Goods Association. "2010 Participation: Ranked by Total Participation." www.nsga.org/i4a/pages/index.cfm?pageid=3482.

The Sporting Goods Manufacturing Association. *Sports, Fitness and Recreational Activities: Topline Participation Report 2011.*

Credits

Images on the following pages are courtesy of the author: 6, 61, 75, 84, 96, 113, 123, 144.

Page vi   Roman provincial coin (177–180 CE) depicting Hero and Leander, courtesy Roman Provincial Coinage Online (http://rpc.ashmus.ox.ac.uk/). Coin in collection of The British Museum.

Pages 2, 3   Hero and Leander from Musaeus, *Hero and Leander* (Venice: Aldus Manutius, Romanus, 1495–1497), courtesy the Bodleian Libraries, University of Oxford, Auct. 1R 5.13, b6 verso–b7 recto.

Page 4   Map by Patti Isaacs, www.parrotgraphics.com.

Page 12   Image of many swimmers from Percey, *The Compleat Swimmer*. Courtesy the Mariners' Museum, Newport News, Virginia.

Page 13   *The Swimming of Mary Sutton*, frontispiece of *Witches Apprehended, Examined and Executed, for Notable Villanies by Them Committed Both by Land and Water* (London: Edward Marchant, 1613). Courtesy International Swimming Hall of Fame (hereafter, ISHOF).

Page 14   Spoon from Louvre Museum, Sully, Rez-de-chaussée, Le Nil, Salle 3, Accession number E11122. Courtesy Rama, Wikimedia Commons. Licensed under CeCILL, Creative Commons Attribution-Share Alike 2.0 France.

Page 15	Egyptian hieroglyph from R. O. Faulkner, *A Concise Dictionary of Middle Egyptian*. Courtesy Bob Brier.
Page 16	Aphrodite coin, 198–217 CE, from Galatia, Ancyra, Caracalla. Courtesy Classical Numismatic Group, Inc., www.cngcoins.com.
Page 17	Detail from "King Preparing to Cross a River (Kouyunjik)" from Henry Austen Layard, *The Monuments of Nineveh:From Drawings Made on the Spot, Together with a Second Series of the Monuments of Nineveh, Including Bas-Reliefs from the Palace of Sannacherib and Bronzes from the Ruins of Nimroud; from Drawings Made on the Spot During a Second Expedition to Assyria*, vol. 2 (London: Murray, 1853), plate 41, page 57. European Cultural Heritage Online (ECHO), echo.mpiwg-berlin.mpg.de/ECHOdocuViewfull?pn=57&url=%2Fmpiwg%2Fonline%2Fpermanent%2Flibrary%2F3ADD60G8%2Fpageimg&viewMode=images&tocMode=thumbs&tocPN=1&searchPN=1&mode=imagepath&characterNormalization=reg.
Page 18	Decoration on Chinese bronze in Palace Museum, Beijing, after *Gugong qingtongqi* (Bronzes in the Palace Museum), No. 281 (Beijing: Zijincheng chubanshe, 1999). Also *Shanbiaozheng yu liulige* (Shangbiaozhen and Liulige), plate 22, page 21, figure 11; *Guo Baojun* (Beijing: Kexue chubanshe, 1959); and *Baoli cangjin (xu)* (Selected Bronzes in the Collection of the Poly Art Museum [sequel]) (Guangzhou: Lingnan meishu chubanshe, 2001), 194–195. Detail courtesy Andrew H. Reading. Interpretation and research provided by Richard A. Pegg, PhD.
Page 20	From *De Re Militari* by Vegetius Flavi Vegeti Renati, Viri Inl. De Re Militari Libri Qvatvor, edited and annotated by Godeschalcus Steewech and Franciscus Modius (Leiden: Raphelengius, Franciscus [I], 1592). Courtesy Dutch Army Museum, Delft.

Pages 23, 24   Digby images from *De arte natandi libri duo . . .* , by Sir Everard Digby (Londini: Excudebat Thomas Dawson, 1587), folios 18, 28, 47. Courtesy of the Trustees of the Boston Public Library/Rare Books. Images published with permission of ProQuest. Further reproduction is prohibited without permission. Images produced by ProQuest as part of *Early English Books Online.* Enquiries may be made to: ProQuest, 789 E. Eisenhower Parkway, Box 1346, Ann Arbor, MI 48106-1346; telephone: 734-761-4700; e-mail: info@il.proquest.com; Web page: www.proquest.com.

Page 26   Advertisement for swimming master Paulin Huggett Pearce from Ralph Thomas, *Swimming: With Lists of Books Published in English, German, French and Other European Languages, and Critical Remarks on the Theory and Practice of Swimming and Resuscitation* (London: Sampson Low, Marston, 1904), 261.

Page 28   *New York Post* headline courtesy *New York Post.*

Page 30   Dongola swimmers from *The Graphic*, volume 30 (1884): 316. Courtesy ISHOF.

Page 31   Courtivron, 1835.

Page 32   Webb from Niagara Falls (Ontario) Public Library.

Page 33   Ederle from German Federal Archive (Deutsches Bundesarchiv), July 1930, Blid 102-10212, on Wikimedia Commons.

Page 34   Ederle's suit on display at ISHOF. Photo by Lynn Sherr.

Page 35   Poster from Library of Congress Prints and Photographs Division, Washington, DC.

Page 40   Fossil courtesy University of Chicago.

Page 41   *Tiktaalik* rendering by Zina Deretsky, courtesy National Science Foundation.

Page 43   Flying fish from J. Bell Pettigrew, MD, *Animal Locomotion,* 1874, frontispiece.

Page 46	Giraffe modeling courtesy Darren Naish and Donald Henderson Henderson, DM. From Darren Naish, "Predicting the Buoyancy, Equilibrium and Potential Swimming Ability of Giraffes by Computational Analysis," *Journal of Theoretical Biology* 265, no. 2 (July 2010): 151–159.
Page 54	Word cloud from wordle.com, courtesy US Masters Swimming/*Swimmer* magazine.
Page 56	Courtesy Sharon Young.
Page 59	"Natation sur le ventre; Natation sur le dos," from F. E. Bilz, *La Nouvelle Médication Naturelle* (1900).
Page 61	Courtesy Andrew Bernstein.
Page 62	Contraption courtesy Charles Shopsin, Modern mechanix.com.
Page 63	Swimmer with aids in Archibald Sinclair and William Henry, *Swimming* (London: Longmans, Green, 1916), 34.
Page 63	Sidestroke from W. G. Douglas, *Spalding's Athletic Library: Swimming* (New York: American Sports, 1894), 18.
Page 64	Quote from G. B. Stern, "Discoveries at Forty," in *The New Yorker*, February 23, 1935, 18.
Page 65	Cartoon © The New Yorker Collection from cartoon bank.com. All rights reserved.
Page 65	"How to Swim" cards from Ogden's Cigarettes, 1930s.
Pages 71, 78, and 79	Hellespont photos by Vural Celikoglu.
Page 83	Phelps: Speedo USA; Lochte: Getty Images for Speedo USA.
Page 86	Ladies racing from the *Graphic*, October 6, 1906, 515.
Page 88	Racing from the *Graphic*, Sept. 5, 1874, 228.
Page 93	Racing from the *Graphic*, July 4, 1908, 5.
Page 98	Underwater breathing from Robert Fludd, *De naturae simian seu technica macrocosmi historia* (Frankfurt: J. T. deBry, 1624), 419.

Page 106   Courtesy James Hilford.
Page 107   Courtesy Andrew Bernstein.
Page 108   Women's Day from *Harper's Weekly* (August 1882): 558.
Page 109   Liberace postcard (Hello from Hollywood by Lamparski) courtesy Marty McFly, SFvalleyblog.com.
Pages 110, 111 Pool designed by Mark Dorsey, Medallion Pool, Asheville, N.C., www.medallionpool.com. Photos courtesy Mark Dorsey.
Page 112   Quote about "Swimming back through your own wake" from Bill Broady, *Swimmer*, 13.
Page 114   Capt. Webb matchboxes courtesy Karen Rennie, www.Rennart.co.UK.
Page 118   Alcatraz swim © Michael Maloney/San Francisco Chronicle/Corbis.
Page 120   Brooklyn Bridge courtesy Capri Djatiasmoro.
Page 121   Statue of Liberty courtesy Capri Djatiasmoro.
Pages 125–127 Coney Island Polar Bear images courtesy Capri Djatiasmoro.
Page 129   Mao poster courtesy Landesberger Collection, International Institute of Social History (Amsterdam). Published by Yangzi River Headquarters, Shanghai, 1969.
Pages 136–137 Getty Images for Speedo USA.
Page 138   Bathing costumes from Marshall & Snelgrove, London, from *Lady's World* (August 1887).
Pages 139, 140 Bathing machines from the Library of Congress.
Page 141   Kellerman courtesy Billy Rose Theatre Division, New York Public Library for the Performing Arts, Astor, Lenox and Tilden Foundations.
Page 142   Beach metrics from Library of Congress.
Page 143   Bloomer sign courtesy Antique Aquatic Americana Collection, Charles R. (Chuck) Kroll, Seattle, WA.
Page 145   Jantzen doll courtesy Linda Dini Jenkins.

Page 147	*The Sketch*, July 7, 1897, 447.
Page 150	Alice Baldwin, Bathing Cap, Patent #1,407,625, Feb. 21, 1922, US Patent and Trade Office.
Page 153	Cullen Jones at a Make a Splash event courtesy AP Images for USA Swimming.
Page 157	Gen. Slocum headline from Library of Congress.
Page 159	"Row, Throw, Go, Tow" poster courtesy Antique Aquatic Americana Collection, Charles R. (Chuck) Kroll, Seattle, WA.
Page 162	Barrel courtesy American Red Cross.
Page 163	"Swim" © 2011 Ram Island Songs, Left Here Publishing. All rights on behalf of Songs Music Publishing, LLC o/b/o Ram Island Songs (ASCAP), Left Here Publishing (ASCAP). All rights reserved. Used by permission.
Page 165	Unattributed image, retrieved online.
Page 167	Flutist from D. Roque Moran, *Arte de nadir y método de bañarse* (Madrid, 1855). Also reproduced in Ralph Thomas, *Swimming: With Lists of Books Published in English, German, French and Other European Languages, and Critical Remarks on the Theory and Practice of Swimming and Resuscitation* (London: Sampson Low, Marston, 1904), 129.
Page 168	"Oh Paul" songsheet, composed by Paul Hosang, lyrics by George Moyse (Chicago: Weaver & Harrison, 1920). Courtesy of the Lilly Library, Indiana University, Bloomington, Indiana.
Page 169	"Don't Go" songsheet, words by William Jerome, music by Jean Schwartz, from *The Fascinating Widow*; cover illustrated by Starmer, with cover photograph of Julian Eltinge. Source: The New York Public Library for the Performing Arts, Music Division.
Page 169	"Handsome, Brave" songsheet, composed by George Whiting and Al Gumble, lyrics by Ed Rose. Courtesy

Johns Hopkins University, Levy Sheet Music Collection (The Lester S. Levy Collection of Sheet Music).

Page 171 "They Had" songsheet, composed by James V. Monaco, lyrics by Joe McCarthy (New York: Broadway Music Corp., 1914). From David M. Rubenstein Rare Book & Manuscript Library, Duke University Libraries, Durham, NC; also in Library of Congress.

Page 171 "There's Nothing Like Swimming" (from *Jubilee*), words and music by Cole Porter © 1935 (Renewed) WB Music Corp. (ASCAP). All rights reserved. Used by Permission of Alfred Music Publishing Co., Inc.

Page 175 Weissmuller from the Library of Congress.

Page 177 Esther Williams: MILLION DOLLAR MERMAID © Turner Entertainment Co. A Warner Bros. Entertainment Company. All Rights Reserved.

Page 181 Courtesy Vural Celikoglu.

Page 188 Courtesy Sharon Young.

Credits for Color Photo Insert

Page 1 (top) Replica of the Diver's Tomb fresco, courtesy ISHOF. (bottom) Replica of "Distant View of the Mandan Village" by George Catlin, courtesy ISHOF.

Page 2 (top) Replica of mural courtesy ISHOF. (bottom) Replica of "Sgt. Kawasaki Crossing the Taidong River," artist unknown, courtesy ISHOF.

Page 3 (main) New photo courtesy Jay Mark. (inset) 2004 historic photo courtesy Starlite Motel, Mesa, Arizona.

Page 4 Hand-colored copper engraving by Allain Manesson Mallet, 1719.

Page 5 (bottom) Courtesy Sharon Young.

Page 6 Courtesy Vural Celikoglu.

Page 7	(top left) Courtesy Vural Celikoglu. (top right) Courtesy Sharon Young. (bottom) Courtesy Google, © 2011 Basarsoft, Image © 2011 GeoEye, © 2011 Tele Atlas, Image NASA.
Page 8	Courtesy Sharon Young.

Every effort has been made to track down sources and obtain copyright permission. If you believe your name has been inadvertently omitted, please contact the author in care of the publisher.

Index

Video cameras
    open-water swimming, 121, 123
    stroke analysis, 89
    swim meets, 92
The Virtuoso (Shadwell), 61–62
Vreeland, Diana, 144

Wait Wait . . . Don't Tell Me (radio
    program), 46
Wallenda, Elise, 31
Waller, Tom, 136–137
Water features, 110
Water pollution, 155–157
Waterlog (Deakin), 172
Watson, Kathy, 115
Watson, Robert Patrick, 63
Webb, Matthew, 13, 32–33, 60,
    114(fig.), 115, 155
Weight loss, 49–51
Weissmuller, Johnny, 88, 174, 176
Whitman, Walt, 165

Wickham, Alick, 69
Widenhouse, Sara, 100
Wigo, Bruce, 33–36
Williams, Esther, 48, 149, 175–177
Wilton, Kate, 134
Witches, 13
Women, 33, 88. *See also* Ederle,
    Gertrude; Kellerman,
    Annette; Williams, Esther
Women's Swimming Association
    (New York), 145–146
Word cloud, 54(fig.)
World records, 88
World War I, 1
Wynmann, Nikolaus, 21–22

You Know You're a Swimmer
    If. . . . , 37
Young, Neil, 167
Your Inner Fish (Shubin), 42
Zen of swimming, 77

Credit: Steve Fenn, ABC News

Broadcast journalist and writer **Lynn Sherr** has been swimming since she was a toddler, learning first by watching frogs in a Pennsylvania lake. She has since expanded both her strokes and her waterways. For more than thirty years, she was an award-winning correspondent for ABC News. She is the author of many books, including *Tall Blondes: A Book about Giraffes; Outside the Box: A Memoir,* and *Failure Is Impossible: Susan B. Anthony in Her Own Words.* She lives in New York. You can contact her at LynnSwims@gmail.com and follow her on Twitter @LynnSherr.

PublicAffairs is a publishing house founded in 1997. It is a tribute to the standards, values, and flair of three persons who have served as mentors to countless reporters, writers, editors, and book people of all kinds, including me.

I. F. STONE, proprietor of *I. F. Stone's Weekly*, combined a commitment to the First Amendment with entrepreneurial zeal and reporting skill and became one of the great independent journalists in American history. At the age of eighty, Izzy published *The Trial of Socrates*, which was a national bestseller. He wrote the book after he taught himself ancient Greek.

BENJAMIN C. BRADLEE was for nearly thirty years the charismatic editorial leader of *The Washington Post*. It was Ben who gave the *Post* the range and courage to pursue such historic issues as Watergate. He supported his reporters with a tenacity that made them fearless and it is no accident that so many became authors of influential, best-selling books.

ROBERT L. BERNSTEIN, the chief executive of Random House for more than a quarter century, guided one of the nation's premier publishing houses. Bob was personally responsible for many books of political dissent and argument that challenged tyranny around the globe. He is also the founder and longtime chair of Human Rights Watch, one of the most respected human rights organizations in the world.

.   .   .

For fifty years, the banner of Public Affairs Press was carried by its owner Morris B. Schnapper, who published Gandhi, Nasser, Toynbee, Truman, and about 1,500 other authors. In 1983, Schnapper was described by *The Washington Post* as "a redoubtable gadfly." His legacy will endure in the books to come.

Peter Osnos, *Founder and Editor-at-Large*